Recalibrating and Other Poems

RECALIBRATING

and Other Poems

Christopher Norris

Parlor Press
Anderson, South Carolina
www.parlorpress.com

Parlor Press LLC, Anderson, South Carolina, 29621

Printed in the United States of America
S A N: 2 5 4 - 8 8 7 9

Library of Congress Cataloging-in-Publication Data on File

978-1-64317-389-4 (paperback)
978-1-64317-390-0 (PDF)
978-1-64317-391-7 (ePub)

1 2 3 4 5

Cover design by David Blakesley.
Cover art: "The Poet's Garden" by Vincent van Gogh. 1888. Art
    Institute of Chicago, Mr. and Mrs. Lewis Larned Coburn
    Memorial Collection. CCO Public Domain Designation.
Printed on acid-free paper.

Parlor Press, LLC is an independent publisher of scholarly and
trade titles in print and multimedia formats. This book is available
in paperback and ebook formats from Parlor Press on the World
Wide Web at http://www.parlorpress.com or through online and
brick-and-mortar bookstores. For submission information or to
find out about Parlor Press publications, write to Parlor Press,
3015 Brackenberry Drive, Anderson, South Carolina, 29621, or
email editor@parlorpress.com.

To keep his errors down to a minimum, the internal Censor to whom a poet submits his work in progress should be a Censorate. It should include, for instance, a sensitive only child, a practical housewife, a logician, a monk, an irreverent buffoon and even, perhaps, hated by all the others and returning their dislike, a brutal, foul-mouthed drill-sergeant who considers all poetry rubbish.

—W. H. Auden, *The Dyer's Hand*

Contents

For Val

For Val

Foreword

These poems were all written during the period 2019–2022 although only in a couple of cases do they bear any clearly marked imprint of the Covid virus or its manifold social, cultural, and existential devastations. If those exceptions respond to that challenge then it is obliquely and in two ways. One is to sustain what I see as the poet's obligation, especially at such times, to address themes and issues of a wider import than those that typify the self-obsessed, navel-gazing, first-person discourse of much present-day lyric verse. Whilst not (quite) agreeing with Pascal's wholesale contention that 'le moi est haïssable', intrinsically or inherently so, I would say that his dictum holds true of much poetry in the currently prevailing US and UK 'confessional' mode. Beyond that it applies to verse that makes a virtue of emotions not so much 'recollected in tranquillity'—according to Wordsworth's hedgy formula—but given voice very often in strikingly inchoate, prosodically disordered ways.

No doubt I'm here thinking of 'performance poetry' at its worst, so these comments should be taken as claiming validity only in so far as they mark the extreme on a scale where force of emotional utterance trumps the requirements of formal structure and intelligent thought. This is why my poems hold out against the prevalent conception of poetry's role in what the philosopher Michael Oakeshott famously called the 'cultural conversation of mankind'. I cite his phrase not for its presumptive authority—backed as it is by a deeply conservative appeal to tradition or custom as likewise trumping the claims of critical thought—but for its power to evoke a very different, more active and civically accountable sense of how poetry might perform that role. I would suggest 'dialogue' rather than 'conversation' as the operative term, and 'dialogue' not in the quietist sense proposed by centre-ground liberals anxious to achieve a placid consensus on this or that issue but in the sense intended by a thinker like Socrates or a poet like Brecht. Dialogue, that is, as a matter of active participant exchange in a process of critical-reflective and open-minded discussion that may just as well be conducted among diverse viewpoints or voices within a single consciousness as between distinct, differently minded individuals. This kind of verse—consider poets otherwise as various as Chaucer, Langland, Donne, Milton, Marvell, Dryden, Pope, Byron, Yeats, Empson, or Auden—has the virtue of taking us outside the inherently cramped and airless enclosure of first-person lyric, at least when the latter becomes detached from the public sphere of intellectual debate.

Hence the second way these poems depart from the currency of much contemporary verse, namely their pronounced formalist allegiance, or their consistent use of rhyme and meter along with a range of more or less complex verse-forms. The idea that such procedures are a curb on poetic creativity—that subjecting oneself to the 'rules' of rhyme and meter can only impose an artificial and highly limiting set of constraints—is itself, I think, among the most damaging fallacies of present-day poetics. Rhyme, especially when combined with exigent formal schemes, is among the most effective and far-reaching of creative-exploratory resources since it is apt on occasion to push the poet out on semantic, associative, or etymological limbs that may then prove strikingly germane to the topic in hand. This is not, I should add, a matter of Heideggerian depth-probing back into the pre-history of modern usage in a quest for some primordial meaning or resonance lost to us through later rationalistic accretions or deletions. Rather it is what the poet-critic Empson most brilliantly showed in action: the kind of intellectual creativity that in effect reverses Heidegger's resolutely rear-view perspective by revealing, in small, the generative structures and processes that enable both linguistic change and conceptual advance. With meter, likewise, any cost in elective or self-willed constraints is more than made up for by the varied possibilities of complex interplay—of dialogical or dialectical engagement—between metrical norms and 'natural' speech rhythms.

The two aspects of these poems outlined above are both intrinsic to my aim of restoring to verse something of its presently diminished intellectual and social-political scope. The formalist commitment is very much at one with the shying-away from subjectivist excesses or, as I would prefer to phrase it, the principled avoidance of any too easy surrender to the more self-indulgent strains of first-person lyric utterance. Along with the more philosophically oriented pieces there are political poems of an activist or strongly dissident character which similarly rely on rhyme, meter and verse-form in making the most of Pope's injunction to 'point a moral' as well as 'adorn a tale'. It's a pity that most political verse nowadays elects either to reject formalism tout court or else treat the elements of rhyme and meter so loosely as to undermine their great potential as satirical barbs and compacted expressions of outrage, anger, and contempt. The loss is all the more striking since UK politics has lately reverted to a state of corruption and hypocrisy reminiscent of the early-to-mid-C18 when Dryden, Pope, Swift and others exercised their well-honed Juvenalian scorn on the iniquities of Walpole's and other governments. While their end-stopped couplets would strike a modern ear as insufferably smug or doctrinaire there are plenty of devices—enjambement, varying line-lengths, extended stanza-forms, polysyllabic rhymes—that allow for the play of complicating moods or shades of ironic self-commentary.

Still it is worth saying that one further consequence of the hegemony of lyric is the idea—more a deep-laid presupposition—that love, not hate, is among the primordial poetic sentiments and hence that any poetry (like that of the eighteenth-century satirists) where the negative feelings predominate must ipso facto fall short of the fully, authentically poetic. Light verse is another genre that can barely survive without the tonal, attitudinal, and perspectival nuances that come with rhyme and meter. Gone are the days, it would seem, when comic or 'nonsense' poetry could function as, among other things, a witty critique of Tennyson—or a smack at the early T.S. Eliot—by way of skilful and shrewdly aimed parody. It too has suffered from the widespread acceptance of 'free verse'—that most tenacious of unwitting oxymorons—whose effect has been on the one hand to discourage 'serious', i.e., consciously up-to-the-minute poets from practising such things while on the other promoting light-verse productions of a technically incompetent and trivial sort. I have included a few examples of the genre here and hope they have escaped the general blight since there is currently a tendency among poets to take themselves over-seriously and ignore—or deprecate—anything suggesting a less elevated Arnoldian view of the poet's role. This often goes along with the lyric self-absorption and the lack of any wider intellectual or public engagement that typifies majority poetic practice.

Roland Barthes once remarked that, although 'a little formalism' was apt to turn writers away from history, 'a lot of formalism' was apt to turn them back. I have taken that mischievously cryptic statement to mean various things over the years according to various projects in hand. What I'd want to say now is that formal devices, intelligently used, can communicate ideas, beliefs, commitments, and—yes—feelings or passions with unequalled expressive force and an unmatched capacity for getting them across despite the widest potential range of predisposed reader responses. I shall be happy if the poems collected here go some way toward corroborating that claim.

Acknowledgments

For many and varied reasons I should like to thank Areej Al-Kafaji, David Blakesley, Gary Day, Terry Eagleton, Torgeir Fjeld, Niall Gildea, Edward Greenwood, Rahim and Wendy Hassan, Rebekah Humphreys, Paddy Jemmer, Peter Thabit Jones, Steven Katz, Rebecca Lowe, Lucy Newlyn, Marjorie Perloff, Mike Quille, Christopher Ricks, Richard Robinson, Jonathan Taylor, Nithin Varghese, and Daniel Williams.

My wife Valerie did a great job of reading the poems out at various live fixtures before Covid struck and thereafter, via Zoom, to audiences home and abroad. She has a great gift for communicating nuances of sense and intent along with salient details of rhyme, rhythm and other formal aspects. It is a balancing-act that I—and I guess many formalists who read their work out—fail to bring off since keener to convey those aspects of their craft or sullen art that cost such a deal of work. I am delighted that this is the third volume of my poems to be published by Dave Blakesley at Parlor Press. He has made of it an imprint wonderfully strong in its commitment to poetic, intellectual and production values consistent with—but uncompromised by—practical or market realities. My thanks once again to him and his colleagues.

'Aerogel' first appeared in *Scientific American*, September 2022; I am grateful to the publishers and especially to Dava Sobel, the poetry editor, for her expert help and advice. Other poems came out on a regular basis in *The Wednesday*, a magazine edited with boundless energy and dedication by its founder Rahim Hassan. Many thanks also to Mike Quille for publishing some of the more directly political pieces on his website CultureMatters, a marvellous forum for activist involvement and debate.

Swansea
August 2022

Toads: a squatter's guide

imaginary gardens with real toads in them

–Marianne Moore, 'Poetry'

Imaginary gardens with real toads.
You need the artifice but life requires
A solid ground-bass for the heavenly choirs,
Or matter fit to freight Horatian odes.
Compare: fine novel-plot with episodes
That hit you like a wave of forest fires,
Or song that answers to your heart's desires
Till world breaks in and common sense reloads.
We poet-gardeners much admire Miss Moore,
Take pleasure in her poems, often read
Them, heart-learnt, as we work, and love to store
Her deft syllabics up to meet our need
For toad-safe zones where we, too, can explore
Life's uncouth shapes from civil metrics freed.

Your toad-less garden rapidly acquires
The look of space unlived-in, formal codes
Unlived-by, all the topiary modes
Of life and art to which the soul aspires
In dreams or reverie yet quickly tires
As shadows lift, as shifting sunlight goads
The lazy gaze, and a toad-chorus bodes
Their hunkering down as squatter-occupiers
Of prime south-facing pads. A time to breed,
And time for heliotropic metaphor,
Like wonder-struck Miranda's talk of seed,
Cross-breeding, grafts—let puritans deplore
Her usage if they will, those tropes that plead
A case no country gardener can ignore.

From frog to prince: result not guaranteed,
May go the other way—luck of the draw,
And so with toads in gardens, though if you're
An adept of Miss Moore's poetic creed
You'll pay the risk of dodgy toads less heed
Than how, well placed, they furnish an outdoor
Perspective and a creaturely rapport
To rough up those perfections that exceed
The gardener's brief. Behold them: plumped-up squires
Of smug repose, squat Buddhas, vibrant nodes
Of brute aseity, prodigious sires
Of plenitude whose teeming spawn erodes
Yet populates anew the bordered shires
With gardens fit for border-hopping toads.

Baffin Bay: a ballad

A traditional game [in Greenland] to predict the future: drops of molten tin are tossed into the snow, and as they suddenly cool they take on a new form . . . . A wave shape means that changes are on the way; an anchor means stability.

—Nancy Campbell, 'My Voyage through a World of Language in Just One Word: Snow', *The Guardian*, Jan 22nd, 2021.

(This poem is a rather sinister fictive take on what sounds a perfectly innocent and cheerful game.)

1

We anchored there, Upernavik,
Way up near Baffin Bay,
Where the snow piled high and the ice lay thick
And home was far away.

We kayaked the archipelago
Through groaning packs of ice,
And what loomed up in the mist and snow
Don't ask, for I didn't look twice.

'Let's pitch camp now, get the tent up quick
As night treads close on day,
For there's many a mind-bewildering trick
These arctic weathers play.'

All night we heard the hoar-frost blow
Like a cast of demon-dice,
For the sound it made was a sound I know,
And that knowledge had its price.

'O love, my soul's turned mortal sick:
Why should we longer stay?
For the wind's a howling lunatic
With fearful things to say.'

We'll press on all the same, love, though
The food can scarce suffice,
For there's one must pay the debt they owe
Now the reckoning stands precise.

Best raise your eyes from the writhing slick,
Best raise your eyes and pray,
Lest the Mariner's vile sea-beasts stick
In your mind's eye night and day.

'What brings that strange, that eerie glow,
What devilish device?'
Look inward, love: let conscience show
How kindred powers entice.

For there's times when fate's arithmetic
Takes over come what may,
When the dice rolls home with one last click,
And the Devil's the croupier.

2

Just North of here the games begin,
The games that now must wait
Till one or other party's sin
No grace can compensate.

It's our cleft futures we shall see
By that device foretold,
Our hissing fissile destiny
Spelled out in heat and cold.

Let each now toss the molten tin
On snow till love and hate,
Like cooling scraps, take shapes akin
To this our change of state.

The bonds dissolve, set atoms free,
Make naught of love's long hold,

As fire performs its alchemy
And fear distorts the mould.

Throw harder, give a different spin,
See how they skim and skate,
Yet still the count says wave-forms win
And anchors scarcely rate.

It's life and death for you and me,
Since you, if truth be told,
Threw one that skewed the augury,
Turned anchor as it rolled.

It's you must call diviners in,
Bid them haruspicate;
My task to check the firing-pin
And leave no more to fate.

For there's runes that augur what-may-be,
That leave us life-paroled,
And there's runes that bring the certainty
Of last hours unconsoled.

It's guilt that crawls across your skin,
So sailors' tales narrate,
Like water-snakes each with its twin
Black vice of yours as bait.

For take a look at the tin-debris,
Those portents new or old;
There's some are truth's sure master-key
While some false tales unfold.

I heard that voice in the Arctic din,
No sound so desolate,
And read the runes till, deep within,
Your curve-shot told me straight.

Myanmar: to the Generals

His words captured the unflinching determination of the Myanmar public in the face of military brutality: 'They shoot in the head, but they don't know revolution dwells in the heart'. The poet Khet Thi was taken from his home last Saturday. The next day, his wife collected his body from the hospital. Myanmar's rich poetic heritage is deeply intertwined with politics. Poets used verse to resist British colonial rule, as well as the previous military regime, which censored and imprisoned writers. Many will remember Khet Thi by one of his famous lines: 'You try so hard to bury us underground, because you don't know that we are the seeds'.

—Rebecca Ratcliffe, 'Revolution Dwells in the
Heart', *The Guardian*, May 17th 2021

You generals, you shoot us in the head,
Though it's not there that revolutions start
But in the poet's, then the people's heart
Where no assassin's bullet strikes them dead.
Let's junk the myth that poetry's an art
For peaceful times, that handy slogans spread
The message faster so it's time to shed
Our poet-talk and take the rebel's part.

You try to bury us deep underground,
Us poets, yet beware: our words are seeds
Of hope reborn, a living force that feeds
The heart and mind with energies new-found.
For it's a precious liberty that bleeds
In Myanmar, a freedom closely bound
To Burmese poetry where sense and sound
Are interlaced with prayer like a monk's beads.

You generals, be warned: we poets bear
Enduring witness, call to mind the crimes
Of other generals, other shameful times,
And—then as now—take our appointed share

In the long haul by which a nation climbs
From dark to daylight and the open air
Of lives now freed, like poems, to prepare
For happier days with soul-restoring rhymes.

It's just that euphony, that deep desire
For peace in words and action that so fits
Our Burmese poetry to offer its
Strong consolation when the times are dire,
But also the verse-melody that pits
Our native tongue against the blanket fire
Of these new tyrants, as those guns-for-hire
Once held us captive to the scheming Brits.

And you Rohingya, you who suffer worst,
You victims of the victims: how shall we
Oppressed oppressors ever hope to free
Our daily lives from an existence cursed
By such demonic twists of destiny,
Such woes long shared yet cruelly interspersed
With times, like these, when closest ties can burst
Like bombs as rival zealots bend the knee.

Still it's the poets, those with keenest ear
To future harmonies, who best can tell
Both parties how to find their way from hell,
If not to heaven-on-earth, then some place near
Enough where our verse-accents may dispel
More strident tones and every listener hear
A way beyond old enmity and fear
As songs recall when that last junta fell.

The Romanticist in Spring: ten sonnets

The analogues come readily, I find,
The metaphors and images of Spring,
Drawn from the poets chiefly, brought to mind
As only nature-poetry can bring
Past scenes to life, recapture everything
Of last year's season in more vivid hues,
And hold in store, for readers' cherishing,
Whatever short-lived moments they may choose
As keepsakes when all nature pays its dues
To transience and it's words alone, by grace
Of poets' notice, that ensure we lose
No detail, keep that vision still in place.
Should I now quit my study, check that they
Stayed 'true to nature', who or what's to say?

Some think my constant reading's left me blind
To nature's endless glories, made me cling
To texts and variant readings, hide behind
The scholar-critics' commentaries that wring
Some paltry point from words which else might sing
A song unburdened by their terms of art,
Unstudied, un-notated, taking wing,
Like Shelley's skylark, simply heart-to-heart,
And so annulling what delusive part
I might have claimed in helping poems live
Across the years, not have the reader start
From scratch in finding all they have to give.

'Should he not venture out on this first day
Of Spring, it's that dull task keeps him away!'

And yet we scholars have our special muse,
Not so capricious, not so apt to space
Her longed-for visits out, more prone to cruise
The textual gaps and cruces, bid us trace
The errant readings, then make out a case
For our improved conjecture, one that she—
No flighty guide—prefers we should embrace
After due thought, when sound and sense agree
And our informed close-reading holds the key
To passages that may have sprung from who
Knows where yet now depend on us to see
By what meandering paths the sense comes through.
Look kindly on us, therefore, should we stray
Outdoors awhile to greet the month of May.

Too quickly you suppose we scholars flee
The 'natural world', use calendars to chart
The seasons' progress, conjure flower and tree
From our old stock, and count ourselves too smart
For nature's over-laden applecart,
Preferring to seek out whatever meets
Our own requirement from the book-shelf mart
Of Spring-themed tropes in Wordsworth, Shelley, Keats,
Or Coleridge. Yet think: their famed retreats,
Their lime-tree bowers, their refuge from the din
Of city life, all half-admit what cheats
Their wish: 'one life, without us and within'.
All's mediated, nothing left to play
Dame Nature to that prodigal array.

It's when they hear of Kant the doubts begin,
When those Romantic poets brave the peaks
And troughs, have their ideas sent in a spin
By the chief message of his three Critiques.
'Each impulse from a vernal wood' bespeaks
Not wood or nature in themselves, but our

Responses to them, what the poet seeks
To pass off as the mind-transcendent power
Of great creating nature, like a flower
At Spring's approach, or arbour newly green
In every leaf, just like his lime-tree bower,
Yet letting on how mind must intervene.
No scene of nature but will soon betray
The serpent's trail, mentation's overlay.

You scorn my studies, mock my office-bound
Researches, satirise my dull routine,
And say—what goes yet further to compound
The offence—that only an arch-sceptic keen,
Like me, to raise a nomos-shielding screen
Against the threat of physis could assert
The existence of that Kantian gulf between
Subject and object, mind and the inert
'External' realm where living things revert
To lifeless stuff, where mind consents to dwell
Within its private sphere, and thoughts exert
No vital power or nature-quickening spell.
Your constant plaint: I have the woods decay,
Decay and fall, no comforts to convey!

Naive or sentimental? Guess you'd opt
For 'sentimental', though the issue fell
Out differently for Schiller once he dropped
The strictly Kantian line and chose to tell
A more exalted tale that turned out well
For mind-and-nature. Yet—much as it pains
Me always to remark—his thoughts compel
A sceptical response since any gains
Chalked up by such all-reconciling strains
Of visionary transcendence often tend
To self-undo when inspiration wanes,
Then fall to wishful thinking in the end.
Like it or not, where time and change hold sway
There's no idealist creed keeps them at bay.

A killjoy scholar, you'll conclude, no friend
To nature, Spring, or poetry, a type
Too often found in academe, who'll spend
His life informing us the time's not ripe
(And never was) for simple souls to pipe
Their native woodnotes wild, for words to rhyme
With thoughts or minds with nature, since he'd wipe
Our memories clean of any place or time
When we attained our glimpse of the sublime,
Some hint, however brief, of what they got
Those words to do: slip finite bonds and climb
Above (say it: 'transcend!') the humdrum plot
Of times filed loose-leaf in some dossier
But junked in soul's poetic resumé.

This much I'll grant, and readily: I'm not
Your Keatsian celebrant, Wordsworthian sage,
Or Shelleyan hierophant of nature hot
For new epiphanies from page to page,
Now aped by countless acolytes who wage
Their puny war on form and intellect,
Conceived as joining hands at every stage
To stifle inspiration and protect
The reader from confronting it direct,
That Dionysian frenzy uncontained
By Apollonian discipline, unchecked
By thought's review of passions real or feigned.
Think twice, my friend, before you opt to pay
In valid coin what passion can't defray.

Consider: how should poems not reflect
What poets read, what vision recreates
In nature's image yet part-recollects
(Ah, Coleridge!) in all that resonates
With psyche's tuning. Think how, in late Yeats,
A strict askesis strives to purge the style
Of pastoral tropes or artificial traits
So nature has its say, though all the while

Supplying further items for the file
Marked 'nature reimagined', one that shows
A hybrid realm with forms as versatile
As any natural kind that lives and grows.
The art of nature: 'Lord, what would they say
Did myriad-minded Coleridge walk their way?'

A Riposte

At the back of one of the houses a young woman was kneeling on the stones, poking a stick up the leaden waste-pipe which ran from the sink inside and which I suppose was blocked . . . . She looked up as the train passed, and I was almost near enough to catch her eye . . . . [Her face] wore, for the second in which I saw it, the most desolate, hopeless expression I have ever seen.

—George Orwell, *The Road to Wigan Pier*

His eyes caught mine, him on the morning train,
Northbound, next station Wigan, me
Up early, jobs to do,
Clothes slung on, hair not fit to see,
And kneeling, stick in hand, with a blocked drain
To clear, the kind of stuff that he,
That writer, took as cue
For telling all the world that we
Poor plebs were padlocked to our ball-and-chain.

I know, I know, all part of his campaign
To shock the shameless bourgeoisie,
To give a close-up view
Of how we live, a woman's knee
On cold, hard stones as just the thing to gain
A bit of extra sympathy
For us hell-dwellers who
Seem so far gone in misery
That, somehow, we've no reason to complain.

What grates when they go slumming to maintain
Their street cred and their pedigree
As our brains-retinue
Is just how often that *esprit*
De parti prolétaire sounds like disdain
For working-class identity,
Or what they take as true

Marks of it, like my making free
To meet his gaze with gestures so profane.

We get it constantly: 'you live in vain,
Waste lives in routine labour, flee
The troubling thought that you,
So long downtrodden, might yet be
The very class best placed to ease the pain
Of age-old servitude, the *cri*
De coeur of your sad crew,
If only you'd promote your plea
With works and days less brutally mundane'.

It's what we hate, that old class-hopper's bane
Of thinking they've a special key
To others' lifeworlds through
Their reading, thinking, Ph.D.
In urban politics, enormous brain,
Or all the myths that guarantee
The many and the few
Won't gel, the few on their quick spree
Up North, the many on their darkling plain.

One fantasy I like to entertain
Is how they might get uppity
When peered at in their zoo,
Those Wigan folk - give him a flea
In his left ear, and then proceed to cane
That book's dyspeptic parti pris,
The doleful tale it drew
From sifting through our life-debris,
Like me outside in curlers, stick up drain.

Give him this friendly tip: next time you deign
To visit, do stop off for tea,
Spare us an hour or two,
And let the lived reality
Sink in, the squalor but, as well, the strain

Of stoic humour that can see
The joke yet still say 'screw
Your Wigan Pier stuff' when the glee
Proclaims 'down south' the jester's home domain.

Please know your nitty-gritty leaves a stain
Of patronage on all that we
Drain-pokers might accrue
Of self-respect, plain decency,
Or books, books, books as our means to attain
The kind of knowledge you would-be
Déclassé types won't do
Much good with till the old grandee
In you learns better ways: alien terrain!

Short View, Long Shot (Zoom)

Short view, long shot: best strategy with Zoom.
First scan the face, then check that row of books.
Let's trust they furnish mind as well as room.

See how the tell-tale spines and titles loom
At you like well-placed topic-browser hooks.
Short view, long shot: best strategy with Zoom.

It helps to think (though better not presume)
They've some of yours piled high in hidden nooks.
Let's trust they furnish mind as well as room.

Unworthy thought, that someone had to groom
That fave array, decide just how it looks.
Short view, long shot: best strategy with Zoom.

Best stash them well away, those *nom-de-plume*
Or pirate texts put out by arty crooks;
Let's trust they furnish mind as well as room.

You've quite a few old favourites to exhume,
Those uniform editions, bound deluxe.
Short view, long shot: best strategy with Zoom.

The bookshops say they've had a minor boom
In the old orange Penguin *Buddenbrooks*.
Let's trust they furnish mind as well as room.

Still who's to hazard what will click with whom,
What old joy greet the bibliophile *redux*?
Let's trust they furnish mind as well as room.
Short view, long shot: best strategy with Zoom.

Pipes, Apples, Nudes: Magritte

(This poem is based largely on biographical details from *Magritte: a life* by Alex Danchev, London: Profile Books, 2021.)

1

One mystery alone: that world out there.
Pipes, apples, nudes, that's all that meets my eye.
Just let those objects claim their proper share.

I've kinks enough for critics to lay bare,
Like window-shards with fragments of the sky.
One mystery alone: that world out there.

I've joys, fears, terrors, horror-shows to spare,
A list the shrinks may work through by and by.
Just let those objects claim their proper share.

He's faceless, bowler-hatted; in the air
She floats, a naked wraith; they signify
One mystery alone: that world out there.

My mother drowned herself, yet if they dare
Say 'Ah, that's it!' my work gives them the lie:
Just let those objects claim their proper share.

So willingly they fall into his snare,
The Viennese quack-doctor who'd deny
One mystery alone: that world out there.

Ask her, love of my life, Georgette Berger,
'Qu'importe ses cauchemars?', and she'll reply
'Just let those objects claim their proper share'.

She knows me best, knows how, and when, and where
The demons congregate, and half-knows why.
One mystery alone: that world out there.

For I've come through with nothing to declare
Bar certain scenes where viewers may descry
Those objects as they claim their proper share.
One mystery alone: that world out there.

2

It's things, not symbols, cover my retreat.
Stay world-fixated, keep the ghouls at bay!
See phantoms fade as dream and object meet.

The critics have me tagged: 'René Magritte,
Surrealist', but who cares what that lot say?
It's things, not symbols, cover my retreat.

Tell them they've got me wrong, Georgette my sweet;
These paintings scatter ghouls like break of day!
See phantoms fade as dream and object meet.

Those Freudians romp in psyche's winding-sheet
As art expires beneath the death-drive's sway.
It's things, not symbols, cover my retreat.

My pipe with riddling caption: 'nice conceit',
That scoundrel Dali said, 'so *recherché*'.
See phantoms fade as dream and object meet.

But I'll not follow on where those effete
Surrealists purport to show the way:
It's things, not symbols, cover my retreat.

A dream of childhood: chest locked fast to cheat
The night-time wish that its stored treasures may
See phantoms fade as dream and object meet.

Then there's the crashed hot-air balloon whose heat
I feel again each time those scenes replay.
It's things, not symbols, cover my retreat.

Georgette has things of mine laid out to greet
Me back from that small-hour *auto-da-fé*.
See phantoms fade as dream and object meet;
It's things, not symbols, cover my retreat.

3

A bourgeois trait, that screw-the-bourgeois streak.
They thumb their nose who've thumbs in many pies.
Of low-life matters I'm the one to speak.

My father gambled, drank, sold porn; I'd seek
Maman for comfort till they closed her eyes.
A bourgeois trait, that screw-the-bourgeois streak.

They're lily-livered, his surrealist clique,
Just tame court-jesters, out to take the rise.
Of low-life matters I'm the one to speak

Yet not, you'll note, at all the one to pique
Their taste for graphic puns in saucy guise:
A bourgeois trait, that screw-the-bourgeois streak.

You'd think their lives were tough, their childhoods bleak,
A mother drowned the scene they fantasise.
Of low-life matters I'm the one to speak.

The 'genius' Dali's just a bogus freak
Who hawks his frissons to whoever buys.
A bourgeois trait, that screw-the-bourgeois streak.

Yet I should talk who watched them take a leak
Through bathroom-doors ajar, the voyeur's prize.
Of low-life matters I'm the one to speak.

Stick your psychology: it's the mystique
My things create that cuts grief down to size.
A bourgeois trait, that screw-the-bourgeois streak.

First principle: let object and technique
Fight demons off before they mobilize!
Of low-life matters I'm the one to speak;
A bourgeois trait, that screw-the-bourgeois streak.

4

Greek drama stuff, yet mightn't it be true?
A hell-bent father, mother's suicide:
What chance I'd skip the psychic payment due?

'The Cherokees' they called us, urchin crew
Of sibling males, maniacally allied.
Greek drama stuff, yet mightn't it be true?

Let's say upbringing and genetic brew
Had equal shares when Jekyll turned to Hyde.
What chance I'd skip the psychic payment due?

We'd do the worst that juveniles could do,
Kill animals for sport, laugh as they died:
Greek drama stuff, yet mightn't it be true?

My art alone, the things I sketched or drew,
Gave me an object-world to take in stride.
What chance I'd skip the psychic payment due?

Don't let those Freudian ghouls bamboozle you,
Persuade you all the action's deep inside.
Greek drama stuff—what if it's just not true?

For me, the world of objects grew and grew
Till their strange antics turned the lethal tide:
Some chance I'd skip the psychic payment due.

My message to him: Salvador, your few
Successes are the paintings that confide:
'Greek drama stuff—what if it's just not true?'.

Take it from me: it's objects pull you through,
Not fears inbred and thereby multiplied.
Some chance I'll slip the psychic payment due;
Greek drama stuff—what if it's just not true?

5

'He painted them away': that's what she said,
My Georgette, when they asked what kept me sane.
It's painting keeps the ghouls outside my head.

The charred balloon, the chest beside my bed,
Their outlines haunt my brushstrokes, not my brain:
'He painted them away': that's what she said.

I fear you've all been grievously misled,
My friends, by critics' failure to explain
It's painting keeps the ghouls outside my head.

They'd have those incongruities best read
As paroxysms of a soul in pain.
'He painted them away': that's what she said.

If I mislaid the torment and the dread
Those fools would call the horrors up again.
It's painting keeps the ghouls outside my head.

Without it they'd conspire to strike me dead,
All other life-protectors tried in vain.
'He painted them away': that's what she said.

Explain that to the Dali bunch, well-bred
As zoo gorillas rattling their chain:
It's painting keeps the ghouls outside my head.

Let them read Freud: those inhibitions shed
May see them dubbed the bourgeois New Urbane.
'He painted them away': that's what she said

And what she knew way back before we wed,
School sweethearts, she who'd never once complain:
It's painting keeps the ghouls outside my head;
'He painted them away': that's what she said.

Betrayals: a pantoum

No faith affirmed without some faith betrayed.
Like lines in a pantoum they wait their turn.
False gods? the ones to whom we lately prayed.
True gods? None such—this truth apostates learn.

Like lines in a pantoum they wait their turn.
This week's high priest is next week's renegade.
True gods? None such - this truth apostates learn.
No faith-betrayer but once made the grade.

This week's high priest is next week's renegade.
They may hold firm who both these titles earn.
No faith-betrayer but once made the grade;
Why then should Judas be a name to spurn?

They may hold firm who both these titles earn.
Just think what price the Christ-betrayer paid!
Why then should Judas be a name to spurn?
God fixed the plot, that villain's role he played.

Just think what price the Christ-betrayer paid!
Ill fame so long as saints and martyrs burn.
God fixed the plot, that villain's role he played,
How traitors fare no part of His concern.

A Point of Doctrine

It may be thought that since there is only one God to worship, a man who worships a God cannot but worship the true God. But this misconceives the logical character of the verb 'to worship.' In philosophers' jargon, 'to worship' is an intentional verb.

'God' is not a proper name but a descriptive term: it is like 'the Prime Minister' rather than 'Mr. Harold Wilson'. . . . in this life we know God not as an acquaintance we can name, but by description.

We dare not be complacent about confused and erroneous thinking about God, in ourselves or in others. If anybody's thoughts about God are sufficiently confused and erroneous, then he will fail to be thinking about the true and living God at all; and just because God alone can draw the line, none of us is in a position to say that a given error is not serious enough to be harmful.

Peter Geach, 'On Worshipping the Right God'

I tell them: 'God' is not a proper name.
True faith pertains to attributes alone.
Most grievous is our fault if we should claim
To know Him as acquaintances are known,
Or as those Evangelicals are prone
To think who 'bring it to the Lord in prayer',
Or in whose muddled minds the zeal to own
Themselves 'lovers of God' must mean that they're
The dearest objects of His loving care.

The merest piece of sophistry, that claim
To be in His good books, as if they'd grown
More intimate as God Almighty came
To know them better, prize devotion shown,
Admit them to His best-loved-creatures-zone,
And by such reciprocity declare
Himself not one to strike a lordly tone
Or count them hell-bound should they chance to err
And fall into some old heresiarch's snare.

Nice God to cosy up to, there on call
When needed, one who answers every plea
For help, love, comfort, sustenance, and all
Our creature-needs while telling us we're free
To dial Him up, not bend the votive knee
In the old fashion, use familiar ways
Of soul-mate talk, and generally be
As close to Him as anyone who prays
To household gods on friends-and-family days.

Be clear: it's now your task to overhaul
Your God-talk, not allow the casual 'thee'
In word or thought, and see how off-the-wall
Your me-you style of greeting when it's He,
The sum of all perfections, whose decree
'Take not my name in vain' your words erase
Each time you treat Him as the addressee
Of some inept locution that betrays
Those attributes you fail to grasp or phrase.

Make no mistake, that failure's dearly bought.
You think me tedious, but I tell you plain:
It's your damnation that you daily court
By trusting through such overtures to gain
God's grace, or through such speech-acts to attain
The knowledge of Him that might else suffice
To save your souls from suffering the pain
Of feeble-witted blasphemy, the price
Of thinking prayerful talk might break the ice.

For here's the simple truth: it counts for naught,
Your love of Him, if with it you maintain
The heresy that vitiates all resort
To human attributes, that constant bane
Of cult-evangelists who strive in vain
To 'demythologise', and so entice
You God-as-person lovers to complain
That we do wrong by urging: make precise
Your terms or perish in fool's paradise!

And yet, as death draws near, I half-relent,
Half-wish I'd not enforced so harsh a line
On you soft-hearted heretics, or spent
Such endless pains to gather your benign
Though ill-instructed flock beneath the sign
Of reason, truth, and grace. If only you
Took this as your sole path to the divine,
With logic as your Guardian Angel through
The Badlands thronged by error's retinue!

You say: too fierce, that old logician's bent,
Too keen to argue, analyse, define,
And fortify the faith with all that went
To armour-plate his intellectual spine
Against how better feelings might incline
If given half a chance. I say: they're true,
Those gibes of yours, yet it's no fault of mine
If over-tightening the logic-screw
Might bring salvation to some one or two.

Revile me as you will, it's for the sake
Of your immortal soul, not mine, that I
Rehearse this formal catechism, take
You through the God-talk elements, and try
To reassure myself that you'll get by
On simple things, like manner of address,
Or knowing just which attributes apply,
And so not have your naming Him express
Some misplaced vision of together-ness.

For it's the worst of choices that you make,
In His if not the truth-occluding eye
Of heretic belief, when you half-bake
These crucial points of doctrine, spice the pie
With personalist ingredients, and deny—
The damnable last straw—that we transgress
His ordinance should we fail to satisfy
The rule that has Him, sole rule-giver, bless
Or not the creeds rule-takers may profess.

Be sure, I feel it too, the mortal chill
That grips our minds as logic makes its case,
As gaunt theology submits its bill
In chat-time lost, and attributes replace
The proper-namester's fancied face-to-face
With God-in-person. Each new point I score
Spells labour lost when every saving grace
Of those I love is apt enough to draw
Such lessons as befit the sophomore.

'The Scourge of God' they call me, one who'd grill
Aquinas and most likely find a trace
Of heresy, or undertake to drill
The Papal College lest it should embrace
Some errant doctrine. Yet the paper-chase
Of academe, that theologians' war
By other means, may be the haunted space
Wherein—who knows?—each new Inquisitor,
Like me, finds their own demon to abhor.

All Down the Line

We slowed again,
And as the tightened brakes took hold, there swelled
A sense of falling, like an arrow-shower
Sent out of sight, somewhere becoming rain.

—Philip Larkin, 'The Whitsun Weddings'

An arrow-shower . . . somewhere becoming rain?
Pure Larkin till, with that last phrase,
It's suddenly for you,
The reader, to work out some ways
The metaphor might do
What, yet again, it does: amaze
You with a sense of things you can't explain
Yet want to, since it still conveys
This thought: if you but knew
How the old misery-guts could raise
The tone, bring off a coup
Like that, then you'd live out your days
Of bliss first-hand, not gawped at from a train.

Each wedding must have been another view
Of what he'd missed, or what he'd gain
If he could just erase
That seaside-postcard, ball-and-chain
Mock-tribute satire pays
To wedlock, telling you the pain
Exceeds the little joys that get you through,
And having him—fat chance!—attain
The long-awaited phase
Of adult manhood when that strain
Of juvenile malaise
Scared witless of the marriage-bane
Wears off and he can start his life anew.

And yet, and yet—the arrow-shower obeys
No earthbound sense of reckoning due,
No heading for the plane
Of well-contented husbands who
Must all pretend in vain
That they've the best of it, the shoo-
In sex, the meals, home-comforts, and the praise
For dumping Kingsley and his crew
And settling down with plain
Old Mrs Everyday. That slew
Of arrows shuns mundane
Attachments, thrills to none but blue-
Sky vistas, other-world communiqués.

He feared Cemetery Road, yet Memory Lane
Held equal terrors; things that stayed
Around for years and drew
Him back across each lapsed decade,
The *temps* he'd wish *perdu*
Yet have us cherish, lest it fade,
In the stuffed annals of our home domain,
The photo-albums, videos played
At every festive cue,
And each bad choice we made
Preserved so they accrue
Like leafless clovers in the shade
Of some malignant growth on harsh terrain.

It's dream-crossed land the fallen arrows strew,
New earth more fitted to sustain
The wish their flight betrays;
To wipe the steamed-up window-pane,
Peer out, see what it says,
The station-sign, and think again
Of all that went so terribly askew
With life and love when both could drain
High hopes like yesterday's
Good news. Few poets more profane

Than him, more apt to faze
The faithful, yet none whose refrain
So lifts the tautened bow: count long-shots too!

His thought, perhaps: should just one arrow graze
La vie quotidienne, imbue
The everyday-inane
With some new joy, some old taboo
Struck down, why then restrain
The metaphors, why not pursue
Each further focal point that draws your gaze
Beyond those metonyms that hew
To the prosaic grain
Of Larkin-land and try a few
More stunners, like the train-
Ride that transformed a wedding-zoo
Into the most sublime of getaways.

The Red Studio (Matisse)

1

Twelve years I kept it, then thought: let it go!
Why have it clutter up my work-life space?
Twelve years I kept it, then thought: let it go!

It shows too much to leave itself a place;
Well-furnished, that 'Red Studio' of mine.
Why have it clutter up my work-life space?

Fast forward and you get the warning sign,
'Set-theoretic paradox—beware!'.
Well-furnished, that 'Red Studio' of mine.

Just see it, all my stuff assembled there,
My paintings, sculptures, furniture, and all.
Set-theoretic paradox—beware!

No installation, nothing to install
Since it's without and they're within the frame,
My paintings, sculptures, furniture, and all.

A piece of furniture, that thing became.
Twelve years I kept it, then thought: let it go!
Now it's without and they're within the frame.
Mere bits of furniture, those things became.

2

I saw it suddenly: Venetian red!
Same stuff, same studio, but with red slapped on.
I saw it suddenly: Venetian red!

First try was pink but that's for the salon.
'Pink Studio' gave those things the merest tint;
Same stuff, same studio, but with red slapped on.

A real eye-stunner, not a gentle hint:
Brush it on thick, let naturalism wane!
'Pink Studio' gave those things the merest tint.

Flat, abstract, monochrome—a surface plane,
Its contents laid out strictly on a par:
Brush it on thick, let naturalism wane!

Don't tell me 'just portray things as they are'.
Viewed without preconception, they're so many
Sense-contents laid out strictly on a par.

One day my 'insights' will be two-a-penny.
I saw it suddenly: Venetian red!
Viewed without preconception, they're so many
Twice-born latecomer 'insights': two-a-penny!

3

They'll say 'ground-breaking—wonder if he knew',
And label me 'intuitive', 'naive'.
They'll say 'ground-breaking—wonder if he knew'.

I knew alright, but that they can't conceive!
Red monochrome, flat surfaces, the lot.
They'll label me intuitive, naive.

I saw it coming, gave it my best shot.
Young Rothko got the message, took my lead,
Red monochrome, flat surfaces, the lot.

It's me they thank, those brave souls newly freed:
Junk narrative, perspective, stuff like that!
Young Rothko got the message, took my lead.

Maybe they're over-keen to count old hat
What I took half a life to leave behind:
'Junk narrative, perspective, stuff like that!'.

Still it's those old conventions kept me blind.
They'll say 'ground-breaking—wonder if he knew'.
What I took half a life to leave behind
Was old conventions, those that kept me blind.

4

Six paintings, one ceramic, sculptures three.
They're all in my 'Red Studio', take a look.
Six paintings, one ceramic, sculptures three,

Though flattened, planiform, and brought to book—
Why let the old *trompe-l'oeil* stuff have its way?
They're all in my 'Red Studio', take a look.

Loved it—still do—that 3-D goods-array,
It's just that those perspectives cramp my style:
Why let the old *trompe-l'oeil* stuff have its way?

Things in-the-round obsessed me for a while;
Planes of consistency now guide my hand.
It's just that those perspectives cramp my style.

No loss of objecthood when surface-scanned;
Things make their space that once stood all around.
Planes of consistency now guide my hand.

Those depths annulled are planar worlds new-found.
Six paintings, one ceramic, sculptures three.
Things make their space that once stood all around.
Those depths annulled are planar worlds new-found.

Bloomsday: divagations

She put the comether on him, sweet and twenty six. The greyeyed goddess who bends over the boy Adonis, as prologue to the swelling act, is a boldfaced Stratford lass who tumbles in a cornfield a lover younger than herself.

And my turn? When?

Come!

—Stephen Dedalus, in James Joyce's *Ulysses*

A hundred and two years have gone by since that Thursday of June 16, 1904, when 'the man in the macintosh' appeared at Paddy Dignam's funeral, and despite persistent investigations and guess- work his 'name' and 'identity' still remain a mystery.

—Jina Politi, 'Who Was the Man in the Macintosh?'

1

Who's come to make us up to death's thirteen?
Who's come to make
     of this poor dust-to-dust
A mystery-tale for Paddy Dignam's wake?

See how it flaps in every passing gust!
See how it flaps,
     that coat, as if to shake
The Dublin dust off all our mental maps.

A minor scene, few living hearts to break.
A minor scene
     yet set to lift the wraps
On sites from Kiernan's pub to Stephen's Green.

Cross paths we must at certain space-time gaps.
Cross paths we must

at intervals to glean
What occult quest subtends my *Wanderlust*.

'Message opaque: press on!' is what they mean.
'Message opaque',
      so I'd much better trust
His turnings-up will show which route to take.

The hours elapse, the chronotopes adjust.
The hours elapse
      as our excursions snake
Their way around those lotus-eater traps.

It's in between that chance asserts its stake.
It's in between
      those glimpses that perhaps
Some stroke of destiny may intervene.

So long discussed amongst those scholar-chaps!
So long discussed,
      yet still the myth-machine
Spins stories, never stops to gather rust.

2

From street to street he must have tacked and veered!
From street to street,
      Hades to Night-Town, through
Dread Circe's precinct and the Sirens' beat.

Odysseus or some dope-head in his crew?
Odysseus or
      the Poldy Bloom they treat
With gentle scorn: his Molly knows the score!

What was it steered us kindred souls to meet?
What was it steered
      myself, the wandering Jew,
And him if not the ground beneath our feet?

Just tell me: who landmarked my out-of-door?
Just tell me: who
        so nearly disappeared
From memory till that raincoat came in view?

A wife to greet as one more *nostos* neared.
A wife to greet,
        though faces showed they knew:
A late homecoming to keep Molly sweet.

All mythic lore when that boy's had a few.
All mythic lore
        and Shakespeare—the complete
Works in his head, eternal sophomore!

Behaviour weird, stuffed full of self-conceit.
Behaviour weird
        yet we get on, us two,
Him the high-flyer, me to tweak his beard.

The name's a clue (what else could it be for?).
The name's a clue,
        leaves Dedalus afeared
Of what self-harm his clever brain might do.

3

I knew his dad, poor Simon, decent man.
I knew his dad
        would thank me to take care
Betimes of his hell-bent, precocious lad.

It works both ways for us, unlikely pair!
It works both ways
        since he, star undergrad,
Has scholarship to help me through this maze.

His part: to scan the magic writing pad.
His part: to scan,

decipher, paraphrase
The text that keeps my daily route to plan.

At times I'd swear it's his own plan he lays.
At times I'd swear
    that's how it all began,
Bloomsday fine-detailed in his college chair.

Each day he'd add new members to the clan!
Each day he'd add
    some mythic name to bear
The coat of arms in which my life was clad.

My works and days have meanings to declare.
My works and days
    gain shape they never had
As he strikes up in his Homeric phase!

Sometimes I can persuade myself he's mad;
Sometimes I can
    believe his talk conveys
Mythemes enough to gird my daily span.

Yes, Mac-Man's there; at vision's fringe he stays.
Yes, Mac-Man's there,
    no soul-guide surer than
That psychopomp in his wet-weather-wear.

4

He haunts me yet, though Dignam's six months dead.
He haunts me yet,
    not Paddy's ghost (no fear!)
But him: same outfit every time we met.

'Just change your specs', young Daedalus would jeer.
'Just change your specs
    and, if he's still there, get
Your shrink to run some psychiatric checks.'

'Take thought', he said: 'you've cause enough to fret.'
'Take thought', he said;
          'much better lend an ear
When tattlers tell what Molly does in bed.'

Mac-Man, draw near: here's consciences to vex!
Mac-Man, draw near:
          here's gossips to beset
With your mute glances, message crystal-clear.

A false vignette those tittle-tattlers spread.
A false vignette
          that has brute Boylan smear
My Molly's name to win some bar-room bet!

There's more to sex than fills the gossip-sphere.
There's more to sex
          Than Aeolus would let
Peep out above the *Freeman*'s lower decks.

Would we could shed that Dublin etiquette!
Would we could shed
          that constant prayer-turned-sneer
That makes such pap of all our daily bread.

What if he's here to help, not haunt or hex?
What if he's here
          to aid against the threat
Of lives-gone-wrong this side of death's frontier?

5

At times I think we're following a script.
At times I think
          we're ciphers in some great
Compendious text where all things interlink.

That's just the kind of stuff he loves to prate!
That's just the kind

of stuff a bit of drink
Has Dedalus spouting when he's thus inclined.

Clues to decrypt through every textual chink!
Clues to decrypt
    with some that bring to mind,
Like Hamlet, home-truths better kept tight-lipped.

Take nothing straight, leave plain intent behind.
Take nothing straight;
    that's how young Dedalus slipped
The scholar's leash and took the poet's bait.

'He's on the brink, like Simon, lid half-flipped;
He's on the brink',
    they say, but let's just wait:
I bet he'll top the bill and dodge the shrink.

All intertwined, they think; a savant's fate
All intertwined
    with that familial kink
That marked them, father-son, twin dooms assigned.

They've Stephen tipped a star, but then they wink.
They've Stephen tipped
    for great things but then wind
The film back and there's Simon asset-stripped.

No genius trait but with high risks combined.
No genius trait
    but has us watchers gripped
By fears lest ill chance fix an early date.

6

Odd, but I've got this sense it's my name-day.
Odd, but I've got
    this feeling I'm the one
In whom today those loose ends form a plot.

Their view of me? Fair game for gentle fun.
Their view of me?
         a harmless chap but not
First choice for wild or witty company.

Scoff as they may, my X's mark the spot.
Scoff as they may,
         my cross-town route's the key
To every main event along the way.

One long home run, this poor man's *Odyssey*.
One long home run
         with pretexts for delay
That let me stretch it out till Molly's done.

He killed the lot, those suitors at their play.
He killed the lot,
         hacked breastplates by the ton,
Dispatched the maids, and left them all to rot.

I let him be, that wild son of a gun.
I let him be,
         that Blazes Boylan, hot
For Molly, she for him—no killing spree!

For who's to say they'll break our marriage-knot?
For who's to say
         this isn't just what we
Two need to keep our demon-thoughts at bay?

Our little son, our Rudy—still I see
Our little son
         who died so soon and pray
That by their sin some good might yet be won.

7

Yet it's in my own skull their worlds perdure!
Yet it's in my

40

sensorium they all
Cross paths, strike deals, fall out, or walk on by

As if they show themselves just when I call;
As if they show
            up instantly when I
Walk their way and remark some face I know.

The sirens' lure distracts me on the sly.
The sirens' lure
            says 'forget Molly: go
To Bella Cohen's whore-house for your cure'.

My mirror-hall reflects no scene so low.
My mirror-hall
            has angles that ensure
No entrance there however low I crawl.

It's MacMan's eye directs the wayward viewer!
It's MacMan's eye
            keeps watch lest I should fall
For Bella's wiles, give lust another try.

Ask what I owe to Dedalus and I'll stall.
Ask what I owe
            to him and I'll reply
'Whatever mind's cracked landscape might bestow'.

No quadrature of Dublin forecast dry!
No quadrature
            but some rain-blessed tableau
Reveals him there, the drifter's cynosure.

My life in small, its star-sign caught just so.
My life in small,
            its private griefs no fewer
But closer wrapped against each coming squall.

Bit-Parts: Autolycus to the Audience

'Exit, pursued by a bear' (stage direction, *The Winter's Tale*, Act
III, scene iii)

*Wanting to be unfaithful to Hermione but consciously unable to
entertain the thought, Leontes' ego defends itself by imagining from
the details of Hermione's joking hospitality that she means sexually
to betray him. Leontes' protection is 'I don't love him; she does'.*

—J. I. M. Stewart on *The Winter's Tale*

Exits and entrances: they're promptly cued
For some dramatic end best known
To him, the puppeteer
And arch-ventriloquist. Our share
To play our parts, from kings or lords to rude
Mechanicals, take decent care
To learn our lines, appear
On time, then do our stuff as shown,
So the good guys get cheered and villains booed.

Call it false pride, or my 'bad attitude',
Or how I switch from jest to moan,
But when the groundlings jeer
At his brusque sending-off or spare
Me none of those obscenities they've queued
For hours to fling I'll sometimes dare
To fling one back, show we're
Real actors, make the parts our own,
Then drop them—not like that moronic brood!

Antigonus: why have his part conclude,
Just when the role had grown
On him, with those words dear
To mockers, that instruction where
His fate's abruptly sealed: 'exit pursued
By [the indignity!] a bear'.
Those cretins love to cheer

When it comes on; then he's alone
Backstage and feels his whole career's been screwed.

All happening elsewhere: Leontes' mood
Of vengeful wrath just lately blown
Quite over, kingdoms near
A peace-accord, Paulina there
To work her magic, the lost daughter wooed
By Florizel, the plot set fair
To cross into the sphere
Of 'late romance', and thence the zone
Of grace where dead queens stir with life renewed.

We comics, clowns and jokers think life's viewed
More tellingly from stool than throne,
Its elements made clear
Not in the harsh distorting glare
Of kings gone crazy, wits completely skewed,
But rather by the lights of their
Court jesters. Fool, not Lear—
That's where you go for near-the-bone
Remarks in caustic vein: don't self-delude!

Reviled, bear-mangled, he's the rubbish you'd
Sweep clean off-stage and thus disown
With the lead-actor's sneer
That says: this guy's one you can spare,
Unfit for wondrous scenes of grace renewed,
So shoved aside while you prepare
To pass through the frontier
Where kingly penitents atone
For monstrous deeds, not tales a trifle lewd.

Let them attain that realm of light, imbued
With all the fake transcendence thrown
On hybrid forms by mere
Intent to have the upshot square
With wishful thinking, or a plot-line slewed

From tragedy to some armchair
Tale-spinner's crass idea
Of worlds new-found or airs fresh blown
From Arcady where no such harms intrude.

My favoured plot twist: just before he chewed
The entrails he, like all bears, prone
To stumble mid-career
Left good Antigonus to fare
Post-haste to court and witness what ensued,
What faked-up answer to the prayer
That providence adhere
To God's design and not postpone
Paulina's fix for evils long accrued.

Myself, I think their magic's best construed
As blather from the blarney-stone,
Or meant to bend the ear
Of those who'd count my bill of fare,
My tales and newsy jingles, far too crude
For folk like them. I reckon they're
The ones to beat for sheer
Thick-witted keenness to condone
The ersatz stuff that mountebank Shakespeare brewed!

Gears: five sonnets

A natural example of a functioning gear mechanism has been discovered in a common insect—the plant-hopper Issus—showing that evolution developed interlocking cogs long before we did. The gears in the Issus hind-leg bear remarkable engineering resemblance to those found on every bicycle and inside every car gear-box . . . . The gear teeth on the opposing hind-legs lock together like those in a car gear-box, ensuring almost complete synchronicity in leg movement . . . . This is critical for the powerful jumps that are this insect's primary mode of transport, as even miniscule discrepancies in synchronisation between the velocities of its legs at the point of propulsion would result in 'yaw rotation'—causing the Issus to spin hopelessly out of control.

—'Mechanical Gears Found in Jumping Insects',
Curious Cat, September 15th 2013

A gear in nature! What are we to think?
No doubting it, the details show up clear.
A standing leap requires the Issus link
Its hind legs, use that high-precision gear
To drive its kicks lest these should fail to sync,
Wrong-foot the launching insect, have it veer
Disastrously off-course, and, in a blink,
Cut short its evolution-primed career.
The cog-wheel turtle wears one on its shell,
A gear-like pattern, but it's merely for
Mate-chasing purposes, or just to tell
The rest 'I'm special!', not to raise its score
In the survival stakes by doing well
And gearing up to stop the pitch and yaw.

Goes for us too, we humans who must strike
A geared-up stance and take its gist to heart,
This latest chapter in the serial hike
Of nature's powers that had its humbling start
With Darwin and now gives us man and bike
Close-coupled, linked through mind and body-part,

Our technics and the insect's gifts alike
The fruits of nature's co-adaptive art.
It's we Cartesian centaurs, mind-machine
Entanglers, hybrids, modes of thought-made-flesh
Who populate the wondrous in-between
Where vibrant matter charges mind afresh
And each new finding shows how they convene
In living forms like gears that smoothly mesh.

No honour lost should we not track the ghost
In body's fabulous machine, not crack
The dualist riddle but have mind play host
To all the cogs and levers, ratchets, rack-
And-pinion set-ups, till it learns to boast
About that gadgetry, not mourn its lack
Of yet more subtle ways to make the most
Of mind's old game and bat the problem back.
Then we might find it no disgrace to crank
Ideas out, lever concepts, get our brain
In higher gear, hook up with some think-tank
To prime our intuition-pumps, or gain
Some major new advance with none to thank
Save minds sustained by body's powertrain.

When Descartes led us up the dualist creek
He left us stranded both ways: left the mind
In self-locked solitude and our physique,
Its outward likeness, slavishly confined
To a dead realm of matter where we seek
In vain for signs of life above, behind,
Or anywhere within range of the bleak
And unfrequented cosmos that's assigned
Us less-than-ghosts. See how they yaw and spin,
Abort their leap, turn sessile, grow uncouth
And clumsy as their start-up gears begin
To self-delete lest they should lose a tooth
In adulthood and fill the rubbish-bin
Reserved for creature-kinds cut off in youth.

The moral (entry-level): junk Descartes,
Re-engineer your concepts, let no soul-
Or spirit-talk seduce you, give new heart
As well as mind to matter, and enrol
All matter's latent energy to start
Res cogitans in turning back the toll
Of minds and bodies cruelly ripped apart
For neither's good lest one should seize control
And rule by diktat. Moral (more advanced):
Get both in gear, let no-one credit those,
The mentalists or physicalists, who danced
To dualism's tune. Have one that goes
'Take partners now', then find the world enhanced
As every mindful thought-mechanic knows.

Of Parables

. . . so that seeing they may see and not perceive, and hearing they
may hear and not understand, lest at any time they should turn,
and their sins be forgiven.

Mark IV, 11-12

We cannot, of course, be denied an end; it is one of the great charms
of books that they have to end. But unless we are extremely naive,
as some apocalyptic sects still are, we do not ask that they progress
towards that end precisely as we have been given to believe. In
fact we should expect only the most trivial work to conform to pre-
existent types.

—Frank Kermode, *The Sense of an Ending*

Each of them makes the parable a bit like a riddle in a
folktale, where to get the answer wrong means perdition;
but [Mark] and [Matthew] distinguish them. One says the stories
are obscure on purpose to damn the outsiders; the other, even if we
state it in the toughest form the language will support, says that they
are not necessarily impenetrable, but that the outsiders, being what
they are, will misunderstand them anyway.

—Kermode, *The Genesis of Secrecy*

By parables alone we hit the mark.
Go wide, oblique or slant if truth's your aim,
Not straight like those who'd get the sense off pat.
Best leave at least some readers in the dark
If light's to dawn for others; if your game
Of hunt-the-symbol's not to see the sheep
Outnumber goats by millions: can't have that!
It's up the Eden-tree straight readers bark,
Their trust in honest dealers that's to blame:
Why think you'll get the point right off the bat?
Let parables ensure you always keep

Some secrets in reserve, don't rush to spill
The beans in one enigma-busting heap,
But let the truth-curve stretch out as it will.

It's truth's long odyssey, that lengthening arc
Of error's asymptote, the traveller's name
For never ending up quite where it's at,
Not having—wanting—anywhere to park
Your nostos-seeking self without the same
Old sense of compass-points that start to creep,
Directions wide of any habitat
You had in mind, or memories that hark
Back to a point just wide of whence you came
And call it 'home', though with the caveat:
'Go that way and your surest route will sweep
The largest area out, a space they fill,
Those quicker options that may overleap
Your parabolic curve yet fall short still'.

That shortfall tells the plain-truth seeker why
It's parable, not allegory, they chose
To share the gist with readers fit though few,
Those riddlers, Christ to Kafka, who'd supply
No four-fold exegetic key, or those
With truths to tell who none the less preferred,
Like Kierkegaard, to have their point of view
Not come across directly, eye-to-eye
With all-too-trusting readers, but disclose
Itself by stages, carrying them through
Successive modes of error till each word
Bears its intended sense, each *mise-en-scène*
Assumes its proper role, and truth deferred
Strikes home in souls elect or born-again.

Still let's admit it's Kafka's tales that try
The patience of a saint, or one who goes
The Kierkegaardian long way round yet who,
When the salvation-chips are down, gets by

On Søren's word for it. 'Let God dispose',
They think, 'and let the author's statements gird
My leap of faith, not have me join the queue
Of pseudonyms, those weaker souls who fly
To some face-saving doctrine that bestows
Both states, the Godly and the well-to-do'.
What's more: 'If Søren's notions seem absurd
To common sense or reason, then amen
To that—faith rules!'. Yet Kafka shows they erred,
Those fideists with their plain-truth-telling yen.

A grievous fault, misreading, if it's thought
To go straight to the heart of things, the one
And only truth, by closing every route
That might proceed by way of errors caught
And held in mind, or insights that have run
The gauntlet of misprision, or—the case
With artful exegetes—the overshoot
Of subtlety that sells intention short
Yet learns thereby how justice may be done
Through parable; how its provisions suit
Our need that text and reading have the grace,
Between them, to conserve what room for doubt
Or second thoughts might yet require we face
Continued calls to wait the meaning out.

Just think how those Romantics fared who bought
So deeply into it, the doctrine spun
By advocates of Symbol who'd recruit
The powers of mind and nature in support
Of their transcendent vision—let's have none
Of those prosaic allegories!—yet base
Their claim on time-bound details that confute
The notion of a language somehow wrought
To such high ends. Read on, and they've begun,
Those tell-tale metonymic slides that mute
That crucial metaphor; the covert trace

Of allegory in symbols that, without
Its aid, would gesture vainly to embrace
The mystic state they strive to bring about.

Still best admit that parables can serve
The obscurantists and the mystagogues,
Those who, as with Mark's gospel, make a prime
Consideration of the need to swerve
So far from plain intent that one who logs
On as the handbook says, or deviates
Back into sense so insights come on time,
Will thereby end up way behind the curve
And apt to call down a new plague of frogs,
Or show they're stuck in some old paradigm
Whose literalism clearly indicates
A navigator tight-bound to the mast
Of allegory that, line by line, dictates
Old bearings, routes and sea-maps long surpassed
(Parabolists declare) as sense migrates
And classic readings find themselves out-classed.

Acknowledge, then, the peril every *oeuvre*
Confronts in parable; how clever-clogs
Or wily exegetes can always mime
Its passage *en abyme*, keep in reserve
All the interpretative wheels and cogs
That allegory supplied, and see what waits
Beyond the next omega-point, sublime
Or trite. Here Godot's messages unnerve
The shrewdest hermeneut and failure dogs
Ecumenists who'd have new readings chime
With old as love's text-ministry sedates
Odium scholasticum. No built-to-last
Consensus but some parable creates
Lacunae and enigmas fit to cast
All things in doubt, disturb the going rates
Of currency, leave no foundation fast.

Take them as parables, those tales of woe,
Of visions interrupted, dreams that fade
On revelation's cusp, prophetic tones
No sooner struck than forced to undergo
Some gross quotidian mishap, such as made
Poor Coleridge break his reverie and quit
The road to Xanadu (now mobile phones,
Back then the Porlock call). Just goes to show,
Like those semantic games that Wordsworth played
With his great keyword 'sense', how logic groans
Beneath the strain of finding syntax fit
To put across a pantheist doctrine bound,
Should it hold good, to heal the aching split
Of soul from body: paradise new-found!

Let parables instruct us: what we know
Most surely is how often we're betrayed
As much by visionaries who make no bones
About the wondrous insights they'll bestow
('One life, within us and abroad'), conveyed
Through symbol's agency, as by the writ
Of sober sense which runs: when language owns
No Porlock-share, denies what it must owe
To mere contingency, the daily trade
Of poetry with commerce in the zones
Of chance, metonymy, or mother-wit,
Then you'll find cracks in any vision crowned
By symbol's vain refusal to admit
What ties all thought to its material ground.

It's in the lifelong run-up to life's end
They draw apart, those symbolists who'd seize
A glimpse of the eternal at each stage
Of temporal existence and so lend
Their finite lives a vision fit to ease
Death-jitters; and parabolists who deem
It best to count their blessings, not assuage
Such fears by some false promise to transcend

Life's element, some angel-eye reprise
Of body's mortal span, but let old age
Pay its respects to both (the late-Yeats theme),
Count flesh a 'tattered coat upon a stick',
Bid soul to 'clap its hands and sing', yet team
Them up as body slows while soul stays quick.

A primal rift, not one that thought could mend
By taking body's part, or body tease
Adroitly out of thought by having sage
Reflection grant how sense may apprehend
Such truths as must elude the devotees
Of *Geist, res cogitans,* or the old dream
Of some panpsychist ruse to disengage
From such disputes by having mind extend
Beyond the human skull. How then appease
Soul's yearning for its rightful appanage
If not by parable's benign regime?
No false epiphanies; accept the tick-
Tock pace of time; and let no punctual scheme,
Like allegory, have scholars cherry-pick.

To William Empson: a verse-letter

*Many works of art give their public a sort of relief and strength, be-
cause they are independent of the moral code which their public ac-
cepts and is dependent on; relief, by fantasy gratification; strength,
because it gives you a sort of equilibrium within your boundaries
to have been taken outside them, however secretly, because you
know your own boundaries better when you have seen them from
both sides.*

—William Empson, *Seven Types of Ambiguity*, p. 284

1

You taught us how to read, they say,
Read better, read the Empson way,
Have every word and line display
Multiple meaning
With all that intricate array
There for the gleaning.

'Too clever-clogs', the scholars said,
'Puts his thoughts in the poet's head
And stitches up the stuff he's read
        With gay abandon,
Like fine cloths he'd as gladly shred
        As lay his hand on.'

You saw them off by sheer excess
Of insight, verve, inventiveness,
A poet's canny ear, and yes,
        What got their goat,
Your special gift to second-guess
        Why poets wrote.

Others had crafty ways to tame
Your errant thoughts, like saying 'Shame
He will keep playing that old game,

Pandora's Box,
With ambiguity when the name
        Is paradox'.

Not so, you said: that's just their trick,
Those neo-Christians, when they nick
My good idea and dare to stick
        Their doctrine on it,
As witness (hear the prayer-beads click!)
        That Hopkins sonnet.

It's why you hated all the 'theory'-
Stuff I sent you, stayed so leery
Of all things French, and found it dreary,
        The new-style argot
That seemed to say 'your tone's too cheery:
        Take on more cargo!'.

You died too young at 78,
Though drinking cheap wine at the rate
You did permits we celebrate
        Your near four-score
And how 'late style' bespoke a late-
        Hour liquor-store.

No doing it without the booze,
You said, the stuff that let you lose
Those writerly constraints, and who's
        To carp at that?,
Though, back in proof, it read like schmooze
        Or bar-room chat.

Had you lived on . . . but why now saddle
Your restive ghost with fiddle-faddle,
Or have you grasping for some paddle
        To push upstream
Against the noxious flow—skedaddle
        Before you scream!

It's as you said, the creeping rot
Of Christian doublethink that got
You so riled up, the sort you'd spot
    When critics spouted
Some new twist of that nasty plot
    The God-squad touted.

You looked back glumly, as the shades
Closed in, across the long decades
To when those pious renegades
    Had not yet spoiled
Eng Lit like all the decent trades
    They'd trashed or soiled.

Forget Dame Helen's Donne, your plea:
Go back to Grierson's text and see
What wondrous thoughts and feelings she,
    Like Eliot, cashed
For cheap jibes and a mockery
    Of love rehashed.

The 1920s: that was when
Your poems tried to do again
What Donne once did and turn your pen
    To making sense
Of the new science, now as then
    In love's defence.

Critic and poet, always keen
To think it through, have nothing screen
That complex interplay between
    The singing line
And what lent love's old evergreen
    New mental spine.

The trouble was, it gave your fans
Full licence to ignore all bans
On reading-in and wash their hands

Of *vouloir-dire*
If meanings burgeoned freely sans
          Intention's steer.

That's how the neo-Christians stuck
Their oars in, ruled 'let's have no truck
With readings that would gladly chuck
          The untold wealth
Of textual sense and have the buck
          Stop where, by stealth,

Those atheists place it, in the camp
Of Donne and Co., their rubber-stamp
Precursors—rub the genie-lamp
          Of poet-intent
And soon you'll see how they revamp
          What's "truly" meant'.

It's why you first claimed Freud as source
Or ally, then pursued a course
With room for no such sharp divorce
          Between what they,
The poets mean and what may force
          Intent astray.

'Dividing up God's Word': so one
High churchman, Lancelot Andrewes, spun
The preacher's task, and so that son
          Of Andrewes' line,
Archbishop Eliot, glossed each pun,
          Each occult sign,

As holy scripture's palimpsest
Of truths that living faith might wrest
From human will and reinvest
          In the divine
Succession Dante-Eliot, blest
          At culture's shrine.

No wonder if you'd blow your top
When forced to scan the latest crop
Of mainly US bids to prop
    The monster-myth
By some lit-crit-enabled sop
    To feed it with,

Or some God-certified device
To tame your errant ways and splice
Your aims with theirs lest yours entice
    The faithful few
To have their mother-wit suffice
    And quit the pew.

For so it was the choice fell out,
It seemed to you: suppress the doubt,
Give wit free rein, and let them tout
    That noisome fare,
Or give the poet's views more clout
    Than critic's flair.

'No meanings bar the sense intended':
Your later view, staunchly defended,
Albeit sizably amended
    Since *Seven Types*,
Thus showing zebra-minds, though splendid,
    May change their stripes.

Now there were books and authors crying
For rescue, reputations dying,
And texts traduced by critics prying
    For some dark twist
Of doctrine they were always trying
    To show we'd missed.

Donne, Herbert, Marvell, Coleridge—these,
Along with Yeats and Joyce, they'd squeeze
For pious subtexts, prod and tease

Till they'd extract,
Like Grand Inquisitors, the keys
        To conscience racked.

You took some pretty scenic routes,
Brought way-out views to fierce disputes,
Took up some scholarly pursuits
        That scholars deemed
Beyond their august institutes
        Since atheist-themed.

They fumed at your delinquent ways,
Deplored each gamy paraphrase,
And seized on every chance to raise
        The touchy matter
Of how you seemed, on certain days,
        Mad as a hatter.

But what most drew the scholars' fire
Was your inveterate desire
To make a case that might require,
        In some good cause,
That quotes conform to certain prior
        Beliefs of yours.

It didn't help—it made things worse—
When they supplied chapter and verse
And you said 'big points to rehearse,
        Long poem, so
Odd slips aren't something to asperse:
        That's a low blow!'.

2

Your US followers soon began
To think you really weren't their man
Since what could more upset them than
        A guy who'd skip
No chance to show the Wimsatt ban
        The rubbish-tip?

They'd seek out strategies to draw
Bad morals that, as you well saw,
Took tips from you in waging war
      On reason's threat
To faith proclaimed from chapel door
      Or minaret.

Make 'no intention-talk' the rule,
You warned, and then be put to school
With any bigot, priest, or fool
      Who lays down his
Mind-wrenching creed as one that you'll
      Take as it is.

In truth the question was how deep
Close-reading goes, how thoughts can creep
In when the border-guard's asleep
      And say: for God
Read Satan, bar your conscience-keep
      Against His squad!

Quick off the mark in taking Freud
On board, you handily deployed
His thoughts on consciousness decoyed,
      Its vigil lifted,
When what it labels 'please avoid'
      Comes instinct-gifted.

Yet it's their conscience begs them shun
The Father who'd torment his son,
Although your rebel souls like Donne,
      Hopkins, and Yeats
Half-thought their lives were a dry run
      For heaven-gates.

Not *Lustprinzip* but conscience queasy
Insists they shouldn't take it easy
But get to feel there's something sleazy

About a creed
That says 'those few are saved, but these He
      Deems Satan's breed!'.

Much better get the poor old brain
To do its work, you said, than strain
To make good sense of some insane
      Belief that turned
Its back on every human gain
      Since martyrs burned.

It's why you urged: read *Paradise Lost*
Like Benin architecture crossed
With all the crazed or passion-tossed
      Expressive means
That artists found to show the cost
      Or spill the beans.

The Eng Lit Critters groaned at such
Vulgarity, feared it would smutch
Their masterworks: 'he's lost his touch',
      They said, 'allowed
His mind to close beneath their clutch,
      That atheist crowd'.

'Just old-style liberal-humanist stuff',
The new lot chimed in, 'fair enough
For one his age but couldn't bluff
      His way like that
Now suchlike creeds are out of puff,
      Or just old hat.'

But let them open any page
Of your *Some Versions* and I'll wage
They'll find a passage where the sage
      Sheds any trace
Of secular-prophetic rage
      And drop their case.

Who'd guess, from that distinctly non-
Revealing title, how you'd gone
Such ways around in writing on
     The pastoral mode,
Or 'genre', or 'phenomenon'—
     Never quite 'code'.

Starts out straightforwardly: the knack
Of pastoral's to somehow pack
'The complex into the simple', tack
     Across some class-
Divide, and let the ironies stack
     At every pass.

But from there on it seems to fill
Imagination's space, to spill
Through every genre-gap until
     The pastoral tag
May seem, text-hopping as it will,
     Just a grab-bag.

And yet, those passages condense
Untold complexities of sense,
Unfathomed depths that recompense,
     By what's withheld,
The *n*th-time reader whose suspense
     Stays part-dispelled.

Yes, 'themes' enough: the tragic waste
Of gifts unused, the claims of taste
(High/low), old pastoral replaced
     By new child-cult,
Plus *Proletkult*, the Marxist-based
     Soviet result.

Then there's your reading of Marvell's
'The Garden' where reflection dwells
On mind's antinomies and tells,

With Buddhist vibes,
A tale entranced by nature's spells
          On dreamy scribes,

To which let's add the passage where
Gray's 'Elegy' turns out to bear,
And—now we've read you—have us share,
          The keen regret
For high gifts damaged past repair
          By toil and sweat.

'A bourgeois poem', you concede,
And thus disliked by those who read
Its placid tone as guaranteed
          To assuage the guilt
That sons of wealth owe sons of need
          For fortunes built.

Tu quoque, some replied: you too,
With pastoral's aid, extract your due
As son of Yorkshire barons who,
          Way down the line,
Takes this late pretext to review
          The mine-and-thine.

They never quite forgave you for
Your point that pastoral must score
Above straight *Proletkult* since more
          Disposed to let
Some bourgeois texts briefly restore
          That rich mind-set.

Make sure to keep them still in play,
Those complex feelings, since (you say)
The simpler sort may soon betray
          The finest cause
And revolutions, come the day,
          Turn Thermidors.

Besides, you got your answer in
First off, declined their bourgeois spin
On pastoral, but let them win
        Sufficient ground
To make your point for you and turn
        The thing around.

It's clever stuff but apt to stir
Resentment, like the title 'Sir',
Which you quite liked but did incur
        Suspicious mutterings
Amongst those tending to prefer
        Less feudal utterings.

This you pre-empted in the last,
Strange twist of pastoral with a cast-
List changed from court-and-country past
        To the new roles
Of intellectual and those classed
        As simple souls.

The *Alice* books bring child-as-swain
And pastoral under growing strain
As rustics pass down memory lane,
        Freud hovers close,
And kid-lit struggles to contain
        Thought's overdose.

It's here, late on, with so much piled
On that unknowing, knowing child,
So many states unreconciled,
        That pastoral meets
Its final avatar, beguiled
        By picnic treats.

The Oxford don, logician, spinner
Of puzzles at High Table dinner—
Who could have guessed he'd prove a winner

At children's tales,
Or Freudian glimpses of his inner
        Conflicts boost sales?

At this point it's achieved a stage
Where courtier's turned Victorian sage
With touches of the scholar-mage,
        And swains must yield
Their rustic place to under-age
        Players in the field.

Behind it all, I think, your own
Keen sense of intellect that's grown
So inbred, specialised, high-flown,
        Or frontal-lobe
That story-time's a lifeline thrown,
        A lifeworld-probe.

You speak of it, the intellect,
As that which marks them off, the sect
Of *idiot-savants* who elect
        To live in some
Swiftian Laputa and project
        Strange worlds to come.

'Hero as critic': that's how you
Described him, an insider's view
Of your heroic making-do
        With donnish modes
Of critic-talk that oddly skew
        The old class codes.

What's 'criticism' if, absurd
As it might seem, the only word
That does the trick, whose echo's heard
        To conjure all
That Marvell's green thought once conferred,
        Is 'pastoral'.

Still it's a high and chilly air
They breathe, this child-and-adult pair,
Each with that psychic split to bear,
        A creature caught
In the same hall of mirrors where
        Life mimics thought.

3

Yet warm things up a few degrees,
Let them swap codes, give each the keys:
Then it's in double irony's
        More genial zones
That Fielding bids the reader: please
        Admire Tom Jones.

Your point: Leavisite censors tend
To come off badly in the end,
Prove hypocrites, or else extend
        Too late the mood
Of tolerance that says 'suspend
        Fake rectitude!'.

Where they were quick to call Tom out,
Refuse all benefit of doubt,
And seize their every chance to spout
        Some high-toned crap,
You said: puts pious frauds to rout—
        Good-hearted chap!

It's why the key-word 'dog' came in:
To show they'd be less keen to pin
The blame on Tom if thoughts of sin
        Weren't so entwined
With deeming beasts in no way kin
        To humankind.

Your joke, but had its serious side:
'Dog' as 'God' backwards, which implied

We humans might be justified
      In saying 'guys,
  Drop all that God-talk and take pride
      In creature-ties'.

Then the earth-touching 'dog' would serve,
Improbably enough, to nerve
Them up, those way ahead-of-curve
      (Since pro-canine)
Avant-Darwinians, for their swerve
      From the old line.

Call a man 'dog' when the Great Chain
Of Being holds, God's proctors reign,
And humans see fit to disdain
      All beasts beside,
And he'll respond: 'say that again,
      I'll tan your hide!'.

Call a man 'dog' when thought's progressed
A century, and he'll protest
With mild reproof or gamy jest
      Since it connotes
'As creature-kind we're at our best,
      Not infidels' throats'.

The thing was, you could rebuild trust
In human nature, readjust
Your value-scheme, and leave disgust
      At those 'dumb brutes'
To Christian misanthropes who must
      Despise their roots.

It's all in *Milton's God*, your great
Rebuke to that bad potentate,
The deity whose advocate,
      However hard
He tried, marked every wicked trait
      On God's score-card.

You took them on, let no point go,
Disarmed their doctrines blow-by-blow,
And let those Neo-Christians know
        How Milton's grand
Design had lessons to bestow,
        But not as planned.

Just lend an ear, you said, don't bow
To a sadistic creed, hear how
The poet's conscience won't allow
        Blood-sacrifice
Its way in having minds kowtow
        To that old vice.

They couldn't drag you to the pyre,
As orthodoxy might require,
And as no doubt was their desire,
        So chose instead
That mockery, not the martyr's fire,
        Stop rumour's spread.

'Eccentric', 'wild', and (standard fare)
'A village atheist'—some of their
Rejoinders, though a few took care
        To say your views
On things like Heaven, Hell, and prayer
        Were last year's news.

It's Empson Agonistes, pitched
Against the God-stacked odds like stitched-
Up Satan and—as if close-hitched
        To his dark star—
Samson and Milton, each a ditched
        Christ-avatar.

You had it out with Milton, locked
Doctrinal horns, your brain well-stocked
With stuff the Godly would concoct

So heretics
Might court perdition as they flocked
        To get their fix.

'Appalling'—favourite word of yours—
Conveys how much the poem draws
On stuff that decency deplores
        Yet cannot keep
From sometimes poking out-of-doors
        To spoil our sleep.

Like Kafka, or the savage heart
Of Aztec or of Benin art,
It tells the reader—make a start
        By seeing those
As not, in truth, so far apart
        From Milton's prose,

And seeing also how the wit,
Wide learning, conflict-hardened grit,
And crafty way with sacred writ
        Are as much there
In Milton's verse as when each hit
        Lands hard and square.

You too, his intellectual match,
Had foes in plenty to dispatch
And, like him, did your best to catch
        Them out in ploys
Not so remote from those you'd hatch
        To quiet their noise.

For him: the Royalists, Catholics,
And sundry other heretics,
All using their infernal tricks
        To falsify
God's word or deck the crucifix
        With lie on lie.

For you: the Christian exegetes,
The tribe of Miltonists, whose feats
Of doublethink required retreats
        To paradox,
That standard cop-out clause that cheats
        Unwitting flocks.

You called it 'argufying', riled
The Christians up, said they defiled
The values they professed, then piled
        The evidence
From Milton's text so high a child
        Could grasp the sense.

Big point of yours: don't go along
With Eliot-clones who say we wrong
The poets if we take their song
        To ask that we
Do more than echo like a gong
        Their melody.

Why should not poetry combine
Keen intellect and singing line,
Though Oxford aesthetes may repine
        At such a thought,
As if choice poems spoil like wine
        Or college port.

At every stage the point applies
As counter-credal doubts arise
And moral conscience, in the guise
        Of Satan cursed,
Tells God Almighty: 'Damn your eyes;
        Now do your worst!'.

You spelled it out, what Blake and Shelley
Were first to say: that Machiavelli
Had nothing on God for tactics smelly

Or hatching plots
To feign some specious *casus belli*
        And call the shots.

'Don't argue back', their doctrine runs,
Those critic-priests who'd spike your guns
By ruling they're the only ones
        Cut out to be
Considered the anointed sons
        Of T.S.E.

For he it was, *éminence grise*
Of Eng Lit Crit, whose stern decrees
Had orthodoxy put the squeeze
        On those so rash
As to think culture's legatees
        Might sometimes clash.

Hear this, the pontifex intones*:*
If you've tradition 'in your bones',
As every grown-up poet owns,
        You'll wisely think
All meddling in such conflict-zones
        Mere waste of ink.

It's not for strength of intellect
Donne's to be praised, for why expect
The poet's gift to intersect
        With thoughts beyond
Whatever works to best effect
        When folk respond?

Besides, I erred: what lies bone deep
Goes further back, requires we keep
In mind the trans-millennial sweep
        From Virgil's ante
To new life after faith's long sleep,
        For which see Dante.

'His influence was like an East
Wind, penetrating'—then you ceased
To join the host at Eliot's feast
        As he ordained
Himself the torture-God's High Priest
        And things grew strained.

For what upheld it, truth to tell,
The standard notion that you fell
Enduringly beneath his spell,
        Was your first take
On Eliot, not the pained farewell
        For conscience' sake.

Perhaps they'll say of you: no chance
He'd turn things round, halt their advance,
The monsters bred in reason's trance,
        When his own brain
Decreed he break Quixote's lance
        Over again.

But maybe, decades later, they'll
Have changed their minds, revised the tale,
And come to see what ills prevail
        When thought belies
Its proper role and critics fail
        To criticise.

Then they'll appreciate once more
How the same mind that set such store
By ambiguity might deplore
        The way it went
With paradox-mongers who'd ignore
        Author's intent.

Puts me in mind of how you gloss
That Shakespeare sonnet where the boss-
Class patron's told: Milord, don't toss

Your gifts away,
Steward them wisely lest their loss
        Of worth betray

Not your high dignity alone
But our small share, we suitors thrown
On your good grace for all we've known
        Of power restrained,
Since your kind seem 'themselves as stone',
        Though that be feigned.

It's pastoral, late Tudor phase,
Where class, wealth, gender, and the craze
For role-play generate a maze
        Of roles reversed
Whose high-low shifts can always faze
        The best-rehearsed

And where the trick with social class
Lets peasant, swain, or worker pass
As classier than the lordly ass
        On whom their jests
Are lost since he's put out to grass
        Or polishing crests.

4

Then look ahead and wonder: what's
The end of all their switching slots,
The country clowns and courtly swots,
        Where wit can once
Again knock rank-inverting spots
        Off duke and dunce?

Or: who's this scion of Yorkshire squires,
This second son who soon acquires
Renown for intellect yet tires
        Of academe
When some trapped nerve of conscience fires
        And feelings scream?

Say: Shakespeare's moody patron but,
Unlike him, not so tightly shut
In self-reflection that he'll strut
        His lordly stuff
Or count the mind's insatiate glut
        Of thoughts enough

To compensate for loss of all
That answered to the human call
For some last chance, however small,
        Of making good
The running debt of pastoral
        To personhood.

For that's the child-cult problem left
In its Carrollian wake, bereft
Of ways to mend the growing cleft
        Between naïve
And sentimental: tricks so deft
        They self-deceive

Both parties, as with that odd pair,
Shakespeare and patron, each with their
Own simple-complex role to bear
        Yet nowhere near
So complicated, strange and rare
        As witnessed here.

For here they intersect, the two—
Let's not say 'different sides' of you
But selves that, like the genre, grew
        More caveat-
Surrounded, harder to construe
        Than wonder at.

No doubt it's pastoral that provides,
Once more, our best of byway-guides,
One that keeps options open, bides

Its time to gauge
What simple truths the complex hides
        On every page,

How aspects of the Eastern sage
Did something, early on, to assuage
Fierce intellect, yet how, with age,
        The culture-tides
Threw up new conscience-wars to wage,
        New bona fides.

'Deep blankness and the whole thing there':
That's what you thought the biggest scare,
The one you might be forced to stare
        Straight in the eyes
If writing poems with despair
        As theme supplies

A way of trading lows for highs,
Like the flat-out 'confessional' guys,
Yet may entail early demise
        Of gift and poet,
Or snuffing some grossly outsize
        Ego to show it.

Also, you said, it grew too 'clotted',
Your later verse, never quite potted
That hole-in-one, outran the allotted
        Count of stanzas
Which often read like loosely plotted
        Extravaganzas.

Not so—that pre-war verse-style chats
And ruminates its way, but that's
The point, a 'late-style' change of hats,
        Not out to plumb
The depths or trounce word-acrobats
        For years to come,

But saying: 'no point keeping mum,
Just giving up, or sounding glum,
Though equally, why beat the drum
        For yet more spats
Fought out again by zero-sum-
        Brained bureaucrats?'.

Seems you resolved: let's keep them stowed
Away in that safe dream-abode
Of scholars, 'bottom drawer', whose code
        (There wasn't one)
You blew with every up-the-road
        Off-licence run.

Re Auden: good to keep your hand
In, technically, when old and grand
Even if the content's rather bland
        And themes now lack
The charge, like close-packed contraband,
        They had years back.

Still your poetic silence gave
You time for other ways to stave
Bad notions off, find texts to save
        From pious cant,
And help drive back its latest wave
        As fulminant

Or else, in *Complex Words*, by showing
Us readers just how much was going
On verbally, if all unknowing,
        When key-words made
Their point instead of overflowing
        Thought's barricade.

It's how you got from Ambiguity
To Pastoral, how ingenuity
Gave way to types of incongruity,

Or the array
Of opposites that your acuity
      Put on display.

Always the fear of how refined
Intelligences might rewind
The clock of progress, how that kind
      Of finely-tuned
Yet *passé* temperament might find
      Itself marooned,

Left high and dry by its retreat
From common ground, the old conceit
Of pastoral with balance-sheet
      Now so far skewed
That gown- and town-types scarcely meet
      Except to feud.

'Good if they're kept from doing harm,
Those complex types', you said—no charm,
Discreet or otherwise, to smarm
      The simple sort,
Yet self-unravelling to disarm
      A rough retort.

Your take on it, 'They that have power',
That Shakespeare sonnet, with its flower
So fine that, should it rot, the bower
      Goes all to seed
And sweetest fragrances turn sour
      As rankest weed.

Poet and patron: one more twist
On themes the canny pastoralist
Could always use and point the gist
      In ways to suit
The subtler ironies they missed,
      Folk less astute.

5

Yet always it's yourself we find,
Those special turns of phrase and mind
That hint at what unfolds behind,
      Or one stage past,
The chapter-sequence, as if signed
      By the whole cast

Of pastoral surrogates, and last
In line the Empsonian critic, classed
Hors de concors (things move so fast!)
      Yet somehow holding
Within himself all that's compassed
      In that unfolding.

Not one to strike the Hegel note,
Though there's a sense, in all you wrote,
Of something *Geist*-like kept afloat
      In the frail ark
Of intellect, thought's antidote
      To mindless dark.

The *Tom Jones* test: it's not the book
On trial, you said—let readers look
Within, get themselves off the hook
      Marked 'hypocrite'
If it's Tom's goose they want to cook
      With holy writ.

No saint yourself, you thought it well
To do without the hermit's cell
Or mind-subduing threat of hell,
      Along with handy
Folk-anecdotes like those that swell
      The myth of Gandhi.

It's Orwell gave a running start
To those reflections, though they chart

Some rocky country since the part
        Assigned King Lear
Of raving tragic fool not smart
        Enough to peer

Beyond the self-deceiver's sphere
Was one he'd played yet wasn't clear
Enough about to see how near
        His own the art-
For-morals trade that let him jeer
        At hand-on-heart

Renouncers such as Tolstoy, types
Whose Lear-like saintly change of stripes,
Or Hamelin piper's way with pipes,
        Drew only those
Who, Orwell-like, changed public swipes
        To self-aimed blows.

Nothing of that in you, no wish
To give up worldly pleasures, dish
The dirt on love and sex, or fish
        For cues to turn
The heart's affections nightmarish
        Lest sinners burn.

Your Sheffield 'burrow' ('lived in squalor'),
Skewed quotations ('careless scholar'),
And waxing hot under the collar
        At God's brigade
All made them think how high the toll a
        Binge-drinker paid.

Still you gave Eng Lit Crit its one
Big chance, right from the starter's gun
With 'Cambridge English', that homespun
        New faculty
That found in you, as you in Donne,
        Wit's apogee.

'Read this', we'd say to students keen
On poetry, 'don't let routine
Responses block the might-have-been,
        The way each word
Or line might now turn out to mean
        Things yet unheard'.

Let's change direction, say Donne found
In you a reader conscience-bound
As well as shrewd enough to sound
        Them out, those themes
Of sex and science you expound
        Contra the memes

Of Christian doctrine or the stock-
In-trade of scholars still in hock
To medieval tropes that block,
        By fixed intent,
All chance that their compliant flock
        Should dare dissent.

Not 'beauty is truth', that Keatsian tag
You worried at (the usual snag:
Those ugly truths!), but still you'd flag
        The lines where they,
The poets, got both in the bag
        The Empson way.

For it's 'the singing line' you prized,
Hit off in verse, and analysed
In pages that leave readers wised
        Or ear-tuned up
To know if they've been energised
        Or sold a pup.

Long ways around they've gone to nail
Your *quidditas*, to no avail:
They catch some trait, yet always fail

Since something in
Your work and life says 'nonpareil'
        When they begin.

Last try: you did what Auden's Freud
Did also—urged we not avoid
The dark side, nor the things enjoyed,
        Like *Paradise Lost*,
From motives maybe paranoid
        With psychic cost

Beyond what, for the most part, we'd
Count off-the-scale yet still concede
May speak to some unspoken need
        That poems reveal
The riven truth our psyches plead
        Some word might heal.

To Val on her Birthday: two acrostics

1

Val, it seems only yesterday it came
Around, this special date of yours, and we
Last marked it with a kiss. Now let the same
Event bring kisses annually and be
Remembered like a moving-picture frame
In time-lapse mode that's made of you and me,
Each May since then, joint keepers of the flame.

No tie so close, no birthday wish so clear
Or spellbound as the wish this verse conveys!
Read vertically and see your name appear,
Rehearsed in loving letters. So this day's
Initialled for all time, from year to year,
Signed 'Love you, Val'. Now let me count the ways!

2

Val darlin', it's a year since you were last
Acrosticked, and you're lovely as you were
Last year, and birthdays come around to stir,
Each year, a mix of happy times just past,
Remoter memories, and thoughts of what's
In store for us in years to come as we,
Entranced as ever, trust we'll live to see
New decades in though chance may call the shots
Off-target now and then. One thing's for sure:
Remembrance of shared joys brings future hope
Revived, supplies (like rhyme) a touch of pure,
Intense word-magic, like those vows whose scope
Stretched forward to say: long may our love endure.

The Leech-Gatherer's Reply

The old Man still stood talking by my side;
But now his voice to me was like a stream
Scarce heard; nor word from word could I divide;
And the whole body of the Man did seem
Like one whom I had met with in a dream;
Or like a man from some far region sent,
To give me human strength, by apt admonishment.

—William Wordsworth, 'Resolution and Independence'

Though old and stooped I do my daily round
Of nearby lakes and ponds, my years four-score
A burden to me, yet with body sound
And mind alert enough to let me draw
A meagre living from the dwindling store
Of leeches hereabouts—a wretched way
To eke my life out, as you'll surely think, not say.

And so it is, and so it goes, and so
Perhaps our twin life-destinies decreed,
Yours to enjoy what benefits you owe
To birth, class, education, all you need
To be a nature-poet; mine to read
The shapes and signs of nature as they strike
An eye leech-sensitised, as once to carp and pike.

No bones to pick, no cause that I should take
Offence at it, your poet's urge to preach
Another rustic sermon for the sake
Of city folk, or else—who knows?—to reach
Some inner state of (no offence meant!) leech-
Like soul-communion with a man you'll treat
As bare life stationed scarcely this side of the peat.

You spoke to me as if to a small child,
Or else an ancient man with whom that tone,

So teacherly, so patient, firm yet mild,
Would least alarm this dweller in the zone
Of second childhood, wandering alone
And no doubt lost in thoughts as far beyond
Your grasp as those of leeches nestling round this pond.

But then I answered, and my words gave pause,
Or so it seemed, to your fond reverie
Of my near-chthonic state, that dream of yours
That in this apparition you might see
The truth revealed, or find at last the key
You'd so long sought in one so near the verge
Of nature, mind and soul where all distinctions merge.

So when I made reply in accents grave,
Not grave-bound, and with words that clearly told
Of wisdom hard-won, thoughts of mine that gave
Your own thoughts back—if I might make so bold—
Then you heard this unlettered man unfold
Such things as left you, poet-sage, no choice
But to find room in you for my subaltern voice.

You'll hear it whisper doubts each time you hit
The high prophetic tone; remark the freight
Of dodgy metaphysics, urge you quit
The transcendental plane, or stem the spate
Of heights and depths sublime by getting straight
About the cost in leeched-out pauper lives
Of those sublimities on which your spirit thrives.

So too you'll find, disguise it as you will,
How often the mere thought of me betrays
That visionary gleam, how spirit still
Confronts mortality in just the ways
That mind, like flesh or grass, wilts and decays
For all your—and my own—desire to seal
Them off, those troubling thoughts we both so keenly feel.

For there's the rub: your 'correspondent breeze'
May bear mixed rumours, suddenly afford
Mind-sustenance, soul-comfort, or heart-ease,
Reveal 'one life, within us and abroad'
Yet thereby bring, through that wished-for accord,
Despair as all the freshness once imbued
In mind by nature turns to flat disquietude.

No blissful dawn for you but augurs night,
That sees love, joy and liberty presaged
In revolution yet declines to write
Those feelings up until they've cooled, you've aged,
And cynic elder wisdom has assuaged
Such youthful fires. 'Bliss was it'—the refrain
Of all whose watchword goes: won't fall for that again!

I answered you full courteously, took naught
Amiss, spoke words that fell upon your ear
As if foreknown; as if you'd always sought
Such witness from the outermost frontier
Of life and death, that zone beyond the sphere
You poets more habitually frequent
Where only time spent out of time is time well spent.

Ah poet, our encounter left us two
With much to think on: me, a life now drawn
So near its close, yet well content; and you,
I dare surmise, still lingering in that dawn
Of every later sunset, endless morn
Of failed endeavour, revolutions gone
To pot, and visions lost as soon as dwelt upon.

'It troubled me yet later gave me strength',
You'll say, 'to think of him, that figure gaunt
And solitary, dragging out the length
Of his last earthly days, condemned to haunt
The dreary moors and hear the urchins' taunt.
See, then, how mortal nature may yet rise
Above the worst of ills that nature may devise!'

Nay, good sir poet, let me not begrudge
You those fine fantasies that far transcend
Not only my condition as I trudge
These reed-choked lakes, but also yours, my friend,
Since all their exaltation cannot lend
The soul whose dark misgivings fill your verse
More than a moment's respite from the general curse.

Think of me, then, and think, if you so choose,
That from my speaking 'cheerfully' and my
'Demeanour kind, but stately', you can muse
Your lyric way to where a common sky
Extends to poets and leech-gathers, I
With back bent double, dabbling in the ooze,
While you—for now—have naught but one more dream to lose.

Yet think as well that dreams exact a price
From those dreamt-of as well as those who dream,
Since you take from me what might else suffice
As getting by, or putting up—no theme
For poetry but, in the mundane scheme
Of things, a fair entitlement to claim
One's age and humble livelihood no cause for shame.

One day some critic-chronicler will trace
The variants of pastoral through all
Those fraught topologies of social space
Wherein we 'simple' people took the fall
For you more 'complex' types, or got to call
You poets down from those delusive heights
To the dank earth where we leech-gatherers fix our sights.

The Extimacy (after Donne)

This ecstasy doth unperplex,
We said, and tell us what we love;
We see by this it was not sex,
We see we saw not what did move;
But as all several souls contain
Mixture of things, they know not what,
Love these mix'd souls doth mix again
And makes both one, each this and that.

—John Donne, 'The Ecstasy'

In Lacanian theory . . . the term 'extimacy' refers primarily to the
presence of exteriority in the intimacy, or deepest interiority, of the
subject, and secondarily to the resultant non-distinction and iden-
tity of the exterior and the intimate or most interior.

—D. Pavón-Cuéllar, *Encyclopedia of Critical Psychology*

'How should such extimacy unperplex',
We ask, 'how bring us lovers face-to-face
With any but the self-estranging trace
Of deep alterity?' Not simply sex,
Donne says, but alchemy that may annex
Our body-souls, transmuting all that's base
In their sublunary element by grace
Of love's command that soul no longer vex
Poor flesh-and-bone. Not so for us who peer
Like necromancers at the flickering screen,
Call apparitions from the techno-sphere,
And make-believe love's puissance might convene
Us two across the body-soul frontier
Where only revenants may pass between.

Donne's lovers occupy the magic zone
Of early modern science where there's still,
In that 'great chain of being', room to fill

All slots from God on down and freely own
Belief in middle spirits, beings known
Through modes of cognisance that overspill
The body/soul distinction so we thrill
To 'bracelet of bright hair about the bone',
His spooky line. Those lovers could believe
In angels half-materialised to taste
The joys of sex, and readily conceive
How human body-souls, too, might be placed,
Like Puck or Ariel, to interweave
The sundered parts lest each grow Janus-faced.

What chance for us to reach that blessed state,
That lovers' reverie of flesh ensouled
And souls whose inmost mysteries unfold
As if, 'to bodies gone', they intimate
Such things as soul alone, without the freight
Of living flesh, is bound to keep on hold
Until, through conjoint ecstasy, the old
Decrees turn round and bid us celebrate
The word-made-flesh. Let us still speak of Donne,
We Zoom-linked seminarians, yet know
It now, for us, a dream-tale deftly spun
By poets, wishful thinkers, and those slow
To grasp how technics leaves the spell undone
As Eros quits the multimedia show.

No making out just when they pulled apart,
When Eliot's way-backdated hunch came true
And body-soul's communion split in two
With poets lining up for head or heart,
Their mottos 'be sincere' or 'just be smart',
And he, our *vox clamantis*, here to do
His rift-repairs, bring off his poet-coup,
And help us post-lapsarians make a start
On Dante's path once more. No myth so apt
As this recycled version of the Fall
To take the fancy of us moderns trapped

In a belated epoch where its call
Evokes our history with landmarks mapped
As clear and fatefully as Caesar's Gaul.

A myth, I say, and one devised to sell
Myth-spinner's poetry to those who'll buy
Such meretricious wares. Yet who'll deny,
Details and dates aside, that if the spell
Retains its power then that's because we tell
A version of it each time we apply
Some on-the-pulses check, glimpse open sky
Beyond the screen, or briefly choose to dwell
On how things were? It's then we may concede
'Some truth in it: a self-promoting tale
On Possum's part, yet one whose message we'd
Much better take back with us on the trail
To a *déreglement* that's clear to read
From this late station on the techno-scale'.

For though the 'new orality' with its
Next stop, the 'global village', seems just where
McLuhan prophesied we'd claim our share
In talk unlimited, his vision fits
This shadow-zone where each new screen-shot hits
Our troubled gaze like some unanswered prayer,
Some phantom presence waiting to declare
Itself one more of those identikits
That swarm the ghost-parade. How else survive,
The chat-box pleads, unless by cutting mind
Adrift from commerce with our senses five
So that, Zoom-guided, we may hope to find
In the next gallery a face alive
To signs of life we thought we'd left behind.

The thing's occurred, far back or just last week,
Whether in mythic form as Eliot
Projects his self-promoting master-plot,
Himself supplying just the needful tweak

To make minds whole again, or when we seek,
And miss, that sense of vital, on-the-spot,
Unmediated presence that we got,
Or thought we did, when we presumed to speak
As living soul to soul. So, while the age
Of Shakespeare, Herbert, Donne, and Webster stood,
For him, as the high-water mark till sage
And sensualist broke handhold in the flood,
We global villagers can scarcely gauge
When each new fence transects our neighbourhood.

Enquire just what it was that really died,
No matter when or why, and you'll find room
For two hypotheses: that we resume,
Onscreen or off, the Eliotic slide
From that lost neverland of unified
Thought, feeling, and sensation with its womb-
Like comfort to us destitutes for whom
The absence leaves a trauma deep inside
Our riven psyches; or that it's the loss
Of faith in all such tales, the sceptic slant
On all lost-Eden myths, the running gloss
That says 'lament it only if you can't
Let go the myth, throw off the albatross
Of your neurotic guilt, and thereby grant
Yourself the prize of getting it across,
That truth, like prophet, shrink, or agony-aunt'.

Recalibrating: a ballad

1

We'd driven fifty miles and more,
The road we took was one
We'd travelled many times before,
A long cross-country run.

I guess that's why I jumped at your
Idea it might be fun
To find some new route to explore
Before the day was done.

We both agreed we'd just ignore
The GPS and shun
That scornful tone set to deplore
Our choice once we'd begun.

The visibility was poor,
Thick mists obscured the Sun;
I tuned to get the cricket score
But signal came there none.

2

'Recalibrating', so it said,
And almost you'd have thought
The voice mixed threat with fear and dread
In that abrupt retort.

We motored on, drove straight ahead,
And every junction brought
A further choice where both roads led
Us home, long route or short.

The satnav muttered as we sped,
Seemed eager to abort

Our plan, like Ariadne's thread
In Moira's shuttle caught.

It seemed to say 'you fools misread
My satellite report,
And took that minor road instead,
That route of last resort'.

3

Each time the voice instructs us 'take
This exit to the right,
Or spurn it for the devil's sake
As those skewed signs invite'.

Still we press on in hopes to make
It back by latest light,
And still it says: last chance to brake
And turn off, come what might.

But I've my driver's pride at stake,
My chancer's appetite
For giving rod and line a shake
And hoping fish will bite.

The satnav screen grows faint, opaque,
Cross-hatched as if to spite
Us with fantastic routes that snake
And vanish from our sight.

4

No turning back—the hour is late
And how should we redeem
Those chances to recalibrate
Our ill-considered scheme?

Twice more it urges we update
Our settings, get on-stream,

While I still strive to compensate
My battered self-esteem.

We see the dancing child run straight
Toward our headlights' beam,
Then turn her head as if to wait,
With us, for mother's scream.

Spare me your talk of karma, fate,
Or kismet—their old theme
Who'd have some occult plot dictate
Her death like Lincoln's dream.

Took it myself, that satnav bait,
Not taken for the team;
My task alone to navigate,
Star-crossed though it may seem.

Some lives may scarcely deviate
From habit's fixed regime;
Ask 'what of yours?', and I'll narrate
A fixture more extreme

Than theirs since one I dared create
When hubris had me deem
That home-run sure to culminate
In my kids' eyes agleam.

Loves and Logics

It is this deep blankness is the real thing strange.
The more things happen to you the more you can't
Tell or remember even what they were.

The contradictions cover such a range.
The talk would talk and go so far aslant.
You don't want madhouse and the whole thing there.

—William Empson, 'Let It Go'

This is a very difficult, almost metaphysical problem: how can what
is pure chance at the outset become the fulcrum for a construction
of truth? How can something that was basically unpredictable and
seemed tied to the vagaries of existence nevertheless become the en-
tire meaning of two lives that have met, paired off, that will engage
in the extended experience of the constant (re)-birth of the world via
the mediation of the difference in their gazes?

—Alain Badiou, *In Praise of Love*

'The contradictions cover such a range'
Said Empson, he who knew whereof he spake,
And wisely recommended we should make
Our terms with the idea that logics change,
That certain quantum puzzles may entail
Truth-values aptly redistributed,
The rule of bivalence turned on its head,
And—as the either/ors begin to fail
Across the board—the option kept in mind
Of thinking there are instances where two
Well-formed assertions plainly contradict
Each other, yet—and here's the double-bind—
Must each be judged indubitably true
With all the proper boxes duly ticked.

The thing goes deeper, wider; asks we view
All human life (the Empson point) as caught

Between such contraries, best held in thought
By agile moves that get us jugglers through
The awkward bits with no balls missed or dropped,
Our footing firm, the watchers well impressed,
And, should some non-dialethist say we've messed
With logic's ground-rule, our reply: 'then opt
For one or other, please don't hedge your bets,
Stick firmly to your clear-cut either/or,
But think: amongst the truths that you hold dear
Are some flat contraries your logic-nets
Won't catch, or some that, once they're brought ashore,
Raise fierce disputes across that thought-frontier'.

Think too: for all your striving to ensure
That no such plain absurdities infect
Your arguments, there's some you can't detect
Since they're way out beyond the scope of your
Occurrent thoughts or items of belief,
Belonging rather to the standing stock
Of those you take for granted, never clock
As 'thoughts' at all, not on your watching brief,
But out there stationed at or near the end
Of a prolonged yet tight and close-linked chain
Of propositions, waiting to waylay
Some one or more of those you'd now defend
As logically consistent, though on pain
Of distant ties thrown instantly away.

'Explosion': Aristotle's view of what
Must follow once the rule of bivalence
Yields vital ground, once dialethists sense
The old game's up, that values 'true' and 'not-
True' may both of necessity apply
To the same statement, though—just as he laid
It down, the canny Stagyrite—not made
To vacillate between those values by
Some change of context, slippery semanteme,
Or other such mere subterfuge deployed

To do the sophists' work. Wreck everything
It would, he said; blow up the whole regime
Of logic, render syllogistic void,
And squander truth so they could have their fling.

No doubt he's right: let logic's dragons grow
Too much at home, take off for dragon-land
Yourself too often, let its bounds expand
To breach your own, and soon you'll scarcely know
One truth untouched by the far-rumoured chance
Of falsehood, or one falsehood not exposed
To the persistent whisper: 'case not closed,
Search further out'. Then logic-probes advance,
Truth-tables at the ready, till the link-
By-link connection tautens and assigns
The value 'true' to statements so germane,
So indissociable, that you must think
Again, re-check the branching logic-lines,
And ask yourself: why not just jump the train?

And so it goes for others, lovers struck
By how their fond performatives are prone
To future disavowal, prophets thrown
By later prophecies, scholars whose luck
Runs out (think Casaubon) when all the best
New stuff appears in German, and the tribe
Of bivalent logicians who ascribe
The rising curve of instances that test
Or vex their precepts to the false appeal
(Note that!) of 'deviant' items, ones that load
The evidential dice to make a case
For dialethism, or make a meal
Of mere anomalies that might explode
(They warn) or blow up in the rebel's face.

Consider Abelard and Eloise,
Logician-lovers, thinkers in whose fate
(The story goes) we read the parlous state

Of logic's world-renouncing devotees,
Yet also—more directly—how they fare
Whom logic has in its beguiling grip
Yet, just on that account, allows they slip
From stage to other-worldly stage in their—
Who'll say?—precipitous descent
Or perilous ascent to regions ruled
By the excluded middle that decreed
No rest for them while all their learning went
To keep two late tempestuous lovers schooled
In ways to quell the body's crying need.

No chance your dialethist might avail
Herself of the old fallback William James
Got by on: 'truth's no more than that which claims
Good human warrant'. Sure, 'the serpent's trail
Lies over all'—the canny pragmatists
Get that much right, there's certain interests bound
Up deeply with so many truths we've found
Humanly indispensable that twists
Of spore lie thick. Yet who'll deny—not those
Star-crossed co-travellers in logic's maze—
What Russell put to James: that taking his
Insouciant view of truth as just what goes
To serve our ends, or cheers us up, or pays
Off psychologically won't do the biz.

For it's a dead-end, not an exit, greets
Each Theseus keen to trust his every whim,
Pursue whichever path seems best to him,
And spurn Ariadne's aid until he meets
A Minotaur whose trail reveals no trace
Of wishful thinking but a lethal plan
Made solid, labyrinthine and no-man-
Escapable except by those who place
Their faith in logic's power to lead beyond
The realm of best belief. No truth but stakes
Its all on what eventuates between

The parties to it as a double bond
Where ego self-transcends and overtakes,
Through love, the singlet soul it might have been.

Love as a truth-procedure: thus Badiou's
Idea of it, his thought that lovers form
A multiple, the smallest, and a norm
Of shared fidelity ensuring two's
The number that requires from each the kind
Of pledged fidelity it takes for art
To break old bounds, for militants to start
A revolution, or for some to find—
In science, mathematics, every field
Where rigour joins with bold inventiveness—
An analogue of how the open set
[*Lovers, truth-seekers*] is the set revealed
By love's subtracting all that went to stress
The singular, transfiguring lives to let
Them grasp the universals long concealed
By narcissist desire and dispossess
The One of multiples unnumbered yet.

Elements (for Edward Greenwood)

For by Art is created that great LEVIATHAN called a
COMMON-WEALTH, or STATE, which is but an Artificial
Man; though of greater stature and strength than the Natural, for
whose protection and defence it was intended; and in which, the
Sovereignty is an Artificial Soul, as giving life and motion to the
whole body.

—Thomas Hobbes, *Leviathan*

Being in a gentleman's library, Euclid's Elements lay open . . . .
[Hobbes] read the proposition 47. By G—,' sayd he, 'this is impos-
sible!' So he reads the demonstration of it, which referred him back
to such a proposition; which proposition he read. That referred him
back to another, which he also read. Et sic deinceps, that at last he
was demonstratively convinced of that truth. This made him in love
with geometry.

After he began to reflect on the interest of the king of England as
touching his affairs between him and the parliament, for ten years
together his thoughts were much, or almost altogether, unhinged
from the mathematiques; but chiefly intent on his De Cive, and
after that on his Leviathan: which was a great putt-back to his
mathematical improvement..

—John Aubrey, A *Brief Life of Thomas Hobbes, 1588-1679*

'By God', I cried, 'this reasoning cannot hold!'
(God witness, it's for emphasis I'd swear.)
'May not the greatest thinkers sometimes err?
The proposition stinks, if truth be told.'
But then I saw the *Elements* unfold,
Found truth conserved, the geometry foursquare,
The logic faultless, and, shown everywhere,
The *a priori* knowledge that consoled
A contumelious mind. 'Such forceless force
Of reason, that which brings us worms to know

Those certain truths thrown up in logic's course,
All set out *more geometrico*
And thus requiring all men to endorse
Them without question or let reason go.'

From that rapt moment on I sought to share
Its tumult-quelling gift with all who'd stow
Their grievances, avert the body blow
Of civil war, take counsel, and declare
Themselves of reason's party *après-guerre*,
Hence resolute to let no conflict throw
Such transient fallings-out into the flow
Of logic's elements as they progress to their
Resistless q.e.d. How not abate
Those noxious feuds, that chaos come again,
Those late debaucheries of Church and State,
When Euclid sets his case out pikestaff-plain
In close-linked axioms fit to demonstrate
Their truth even to my befuddled brain.

I wrote my book *Leviathan* to teach
Those sectaries the error of their ways,
To lead them by example through the maze
Of falsehoods spread by zealots out to preach
Sedition and the anarch's code of each
Man his own conscience, qualified to raise
A schism, creed, or army, or—in days
Not long gone by—a monstrous gaping breach
In reason's commonwealth. Let *civis* learn
From geometer not prelate, statesman take
A course in axiomatics, preacher turn
To Euclid for instruction—then they'll make
Good all the damage done by those who spurn
The way of truth for private passion's sake.

Truth absolute, indubitable, shown
By formal proof, and thereby proof against
Mob sentiment, unreason, brains incensed

By ranting oratory, rebellion grown
To compass regicide—it's that alone,
That one sure anchor-point, that recompensed
The ages of stupidity condensed
In the phrase 'civil war' whose gist I groan
Once more to recollect. A forlorn hope,
I sometimes think, my bookish quest to coax
The zealots down, have calmer passions cope
In such wild times when reason's voice provokes
Rekindled strife. Yet soon enough I'll grope
My next inch forward despite the taunts and jokes.

They're prey to phantasms, to all the tricks
And shape-shift sorceries that craze the mind
When Proteus meddles with the laws of kind,
Sets men at odds, confounds their politics,
And visits on them that unholy mix
Of party, faith and avarice combined
That leaves Leviathan compelled to find,
Sans sovereign reason, other ways to fix
Its storm-tossed voyaging. Then, to be sure,
Unending motion holds the only key
To minds as well as bodies; thoughts endure
No more than shapes or sizes, and if we
Think otherwise it's only till the lure
Of motion drives us whales back out to sea.

My death draws nigh and says 'Don't be afraid',
Which counsel now, *aetatis* eighty-four,
I take to heart and cherish all the more
For having lived by reason's light and made,
As best I could, its rule the one that weighed
Most strongly with me since inclined to draw,
In those my books, sound lessons from the store
Of ancient precedents now aptly laid
Before our warring tribes. As bodies yield
To intellect, so they must yield to laws
Prescribed, and rightly so, by those who wield

The sovereign power to separate just cause
From unjust, act as Everyman's best shield,
And keep Leviathan from Satan's jaws.

To Malmesbury I'll soon return and die,
Perhaps, with childhood landmarks clear in view,
The ancient monastery and castle, two
Fine citadels of Church and State, set high
On that opposing hillside and, to my
Mind even then, each with its power to do
Great good or harm; trust reason and stay true
To virtue's cause or further amplify
Our discords lately quelled. For nothing stirs
The blood to faction, feud and all the woes
Of civil war like powers abused, nor spurs
The virtuous mind more firmly to oppose
War's evils than the insight that confers
Such peace as civic geometry bestows.

Yet I've no ready answer, none to quiet
Their taunts or my own doubts, when sceptics mock
My thought that Euclid's proofs might ease the shock
Of civil strife, cool hotheads ere they riot,
Bring social peace through change of mental diet,
Or—sheer absurdity!—provide a rock
Of shared assent for those inclined to knock
The block off any party who won't buy it
When they dictate what's what. And there's the fact,
Much dwelt on by those carpers, that so far
From lying low, preferring thought to act,
And hiding in my study lest I mar
The Euclid moment, I've at no time lacked
For worldly ways to chase Dame Fortune's star.

Nor should they count me fool enough to think
It might, that moment, somehow overleap
The confine of my skull and swiftly creep,
As if by occult medium, link by link,

Into the skulls of those caught on the brink
Of civil war, contriving thus to keep
Their nations free of all that else might sweep
Whole polities to limbo in a blink
Of its Cyclopic eye. What might the name
'Hobbes' signify, in popular repute,
If not the wicked infidel whose aim
Is to relinquish mind and soul to brute
Materiality, and who'd proclaim
Such mystic notions kids' stuff to refute?

That gets me wrong, flat wrong, but I'll concede
One point: there's no royal road, nor (if you please)
Republican thought-highway fit to ease
My contrarieties, my twofold need
That civic order take the form decreed
By reason's rule and, as I see in these
Bad times, that no fake nostrum claim to ease
The restless passions chafing to stampede
In all men, me not least. They'll read my works
In times to come, those scholars, and enquire
What demon drove me on, what tumult lurks
Behind the Euclid-tale they so admire,
Or why that soothing anecdote still irks
One lured as much by reason as desire.

Seasonal: two verse-polemics

1 BoJo: a litany

I hate your lies, the monstrous lot
Of lies you've told to save your skin,
To line your pockets, take a shot
At some old rival, seek to pin
The blame elsewhere, pretend you've got
A half-way truthful tale to spin,
Or tell the world you're really not
That scheming bastard out to win
A bit more time before the plot
Unravels and you end up in
Deep shit, or gaol, or a tight spot
Where your glib tongue and oafish grin
Won't ease the punishment one jot
Or help you take it on the chin.

I hate your fake patrician ways,
Your indolence, your languid drawl,
Your mindless yawp, your fool displays
Of boorishness, your flaccid sprawl
On that front bench, the way they glaze,
Those eyes of yours, when some close call
Gets through at Question Time, the maze
Of lies, brush-offs, attempts to stall
For time, or feeble jokes to raise
A laugh from crass back-benchers—all
These things I hate, and count the days
Until at last the blinkers fall,
You're naked in the public gaze
And off to gaol for the long haul.

I hate your Eton-Oxford-primed veneer

Of civilized behavior, wit,
And what does service in that sphere
As intellect, though scarcely fit
To hide your lack of mental gear,
Your fallback mode of trueborn Brit
With speech to prove it: Eton sneer
Or Oxford posh, the standard kit
For those whose choices of career –
Say, politics or crime—admit
No end of vicious traits or sheer
Stupidity but tell them 'quit!'
If class and breeding don't appear
Quite right to make their role legit.

Another thing I hate: how your
Vile defects all bespeak the same
Root vice, how rot infects the core
Of BoJo-being, how your name
Alone's enough for us to score
A moral bull's-eye—lack of shame,
The crook's last alibi, the store
Of handy get-outs when the game
Goes wrong, the fraudster's bottom drawer
Of killer notes to help defame
Some pesky journalist or shore
Your last defences up when blame,
At last, lies squarely at your door
And justice comes to stake its claim.

But, truth to tell, what I most hate
Is how those COVID victims died
In tens of thousands, how the rate
Sky-rocketed because you tried
To fix the numbers, under-state
The risks, keep your rich chums onside,
Give each big contract to some mate

Of yours with zero bona fide,
Put lockdowns off till it's too late,
Bluff your way through, let COVID ride,
Leave care-home dwellers to their fate,
Make sure the tabloid hacks provide
Your cover, then sit back and wait
As each new variant hits its stride.

2. The Bodyguard's Tale

You can call me his chief protector,
You can call me his hired gun,
You can call me Chief Inspector
Since it's one of the jobs I've done.
Started off in the private sector,
Looking out for Number One –
I'd have taken on Hannibal Lecter
With the bunch I used to run!
Then I joined the Old Bill as Director
Of Ops for his days in the sun
When we'd duff up the odd objector
While the monster was out having fun.

Yet I thought: who'd be poacher-turned-keeper
If 'security' means you're employed
Just to shelter this jerk from the Reaper,
This cock of the walk who's destroyed
Human lives by the thousand (much cheaper
Than the health-care he enjoyed!),
Whose lies twist and cling like a creeper,
Whose stunts are pure celluloid,
And whose harms to the country strike deeper
Than a germ-bearing asteroid.

Then I thought: what are bodyguards there for
In such desperate times as these
When the top guy we're summoned to care for
Has brought the whole land to its knees?
It's not monsters like him we prepare for,
Not scoundrels who loll at their ease
While the people they've no time to spare for
Die in droves from a viral disease
And the 'freedom' he wants a fanfare for
Is the freedom to die as we please.

A dilemma, but soon I decided
Where my best course of action lay
If this old hired gun were now guided
To bring predator down, not prey.
Oh, the papers will feast on it: 'why did
Such a cool hand as him go astray?',
And I'll tell them: 'It's one thing I've prided
Myself on—still having the say
When duty and right are divided
And duty just has to give way'.

No denying the hour was a sad one
When conscience submitted its plea
And I thought: 'Career? You once had one,
With your hiked-up protection fee.
But this last guy turned out such a bad one
That you shook the poison-tree!'.
So I'd practise the hip-shots, then add one,
Get the whole thing worked out to a tee,
With the monster's last outing a mad one
Facing all his accusers in me.

Unseasonal

Across Britain, the woods are turning orange. Drifts of dry leaves are growing on forest floors and eddying into street corners. Hawthorn and rowan, elder and holly berries are all ripening, and the ferns are fringes of gold. From a distance, it is beautiful. But the air is still warm and summery.

And all of it is two or three months early . . . . This turning and leaf fall is not the usual gradual preparation for winter in temperate zones but a stress response by trees trying to conserve water. We are now in a false autumn, caused by heat and drought. And it feels wrong.

—Editorial (unsigned), *The Guardian*, August 28th 2022

Mid-Summer still, yet all the leaves are sere,
Cast down already by the slightest breeze,
And telling us the seasons of the year
Must even now be shifting by degrees.

Late-July blackberries: a sight to cheer
Suburban folk who gather as they please,
Though best make haste lest berries disappear
Too soon, along with pollinating bees.

See how the branches wither, sag and shear
As the sap sinks in desiccated trees
And leaf-protected nests now show up clear
Through the sun-fretted witches'-knitting frieze.

Now we've new birds that make first landfall here,
El-Niño-borne across far lands and seas,
Though it's no instinct-driven course they steer
Nor bound to nature's seasonal decrees.

For chaos grows throughout the troposphere
And they, like all things living, feel the squeeze
As Jet-Stream currents buck, old flight-paths veer,
And the new climate-gods are hard to please.

Once Bible-bashers said 'The end is near!',
And they alone had charge of heaven's keys,
But now we're all in the same boat, I fear,
And bailing out on hands as well as knees.

'It's Summer still, why pack your Autumn gear?'
The hopers say, but show distinct unease
As old doom-merchants get their chance to jeer
Like medics at some long-concealed disease.

Now ice-caps thaw and melting snows career
Down mountainsides while all the indices
Say 'Lord, it is time, the Summer was too queer,
Too stifling hot: let Autumn now appease

Great Gaia or the gods who tell us we're
Destruction-bound since all our madcap sprees
Have brought us out slap on the last frontier
Where heat tears up all life-time guarantees.

Time was when we had Keats, Romantic fellow,
Whose wondrous 'Ode to Autumn' hymned the season
As that of soul-enchanting 'mists and mellow
Fruitfulness', though these days we've every reason
To change our tune as all the greens turn yellow,
Bright petals bleach and fall, no flowers have bees on,
And dark-hued keys in nature's ritornello
Have the whole works to lay their minor keys on.

Who's then the nature-poet fit to speak
For us, poor legatees of all that's screwed
Our lifeworld up so now we're left to seek
Some world elsewhere, some better life as viewed

From way upstream beyond the fetid creek
We're stuck in. Think of it, the stuff accrued
Since Blake first conjured poetry's mystique
Against the devil commerce and its brood

Of vandals and polluters out to leak,
Offload, combust, or belch a multitude
Of harms now stretching to the highest peak
Of Wordsworth's cloud-capped vision, or imbued

Indelibly in every spectral streak
Of foiled intent through which the poet's mood,
Ut pictura poesis, went oblique
Ways round to show how nothing might elude

The creeping nature-blight. What vision bleak,
Crepuscular enough to offer food
For soul-starved hungers, appetites left weak
By spirit's inanition, feelings wooed

To rest content with all that verse-technique
Can do (as here, you may think) to exude
At least some distant kinship to a clique
Of High-Romantic visionaries endued,

Back then, with all that our lot have to eke
Out fretfully from nature's signs construed
As last reminders of its power to wreak
Fresh chaos with each heat-alert renewed.

The Fifth Horseman

Fifth Horseman, that's the job for me,
The one they sent ahead
To speed catastrophe and see
All living creatures dead.

The Bible said 'These things shall be;
Await God's wrath with dread',
But my old stable-mates agree:
Let's speed things up instead!

We've Earthly allies on a spree,
All looking sharp to spread
The message: help yourselves, feel free,
Let queasy qualms be shed!

It's growing hedge-funds, that's the key,
Not all that daily-bread
Stuff they despise, the powers-that-be,
So long as they're well-fed.

We've paid the lawyer-crooks their fee,
All tucked up tight in bed
With ministers who tell them: 'We
Have documents to shred'.

We've got the top politicos
All stashing cash galore
From oil tycoons and CEOs
With bank accounts offshore.

We've got MPs whose fortune grows
On every trading-floor
With yet more juicy deals to close
Once through the revolving door.

We've got the tabloid hacks we chose
To wage our covert war
On anyone who dared oppose
The might of Fracking Corp'.

We've got a government that knows
The stuff we're looking for,
Like making sure the money flows
To stinking-rich, not poor.

And then we've got what really shows
We know the Doomsday score:
Our trusty bunch who'll hold their nose
Whatever shit's in store.

But most importantly we've got
The Tories well onside:
They talk green but they've told our lot
Don't fret—tax-breaks supplied!

They'll slash those taxes on the dot,
Consult the Frackers' Guide,
And tell the plebs: 'You're feeling hot?
Just eat your chips deep-fried'.

They'll stop all that 'green levy' rot
And spread the message wide:
Keep filling the old money-pot
And stretch the wealth-divide!

They'll give the paupers diddly-squat
Except to feel the slide
From pauperdom to their last spot
Of shade: no place to hide.

Fires, floods and famine on the trot—
That's what our team provide,

And they're the ones to see it's not
Apocalypse we're denied.

No copy-book they'll fail to blot,
No lie they won't abide
To give Doomsday a booster-shot
And see us horsemen ride.

Passions of the Cogito

Note: this imaginary dialogue concerns Descartes' visit to the court of Queen Christina of Sweden, a person of extraordinary gifts, intellectual achievements, and life-historical vicissitudes. It also concerns Descartes' (to say the least) problematic doctrine of mind-body dualism and, more specifically, the difficulties this creates when taken in conjunction with his treatise *The Passions of the Soul*. His death during the visit—perhaps attributable in part to the intensely cold Swedish winter—is also conceived (with due fictive licence) as being somehow related to the conjoint strains of his pedagogical-erotic relationship with Christina and the tension within his philosophical project brought to breaking-point by that relationship.

Christina

We sought each other out yet now go ways
Around to put off meeting, steer
Some devious paths to keep
Our mental realms distinct and clear,
Our well-attuned sensoria out-of-phase
Enough to quell the rising fear
Lest glances overleap
The ego-boundaries that we're
Each subject to, we thought-locked *émigrés*.

Years long we corresponded, thoughts so deep,
So strange and subtle that for days
On end I'd persevere
With some hard passage, some odd phrase
Of his that came to me betimes in sleep
With yet more searching doubts to raise,
New demons set to jeer
At each new card that reason plays
From its well-thumbed and trickster-shuffled heap.

I craved he visit me, but now he's here
We find ourselves compelled to creep

About and lift our gaze
Lest, should eyes meet, some demon peep
From soul to soul, invade the crystal sphere
Of intellect, and quickly sweep
Mind's ramparts down to craze
Us both with monstrous thoughts that seep
Through every chink till giant cracks appear.

RD

You see me now a marked man, hunted through
The many lands of Europe where
My writings most dismayed
Those guardians of the faith whose share
Of Man's God-given reason failed to do
What it has done for me—declare
The certain knowledge laid
Up in each soul by thoughts that bear
First-person witness, each time vouched anew.

And yet I see it's making you afraid,
You bravest of your sex, when you
Raise doubts and I prepare
My answer, then fresh doubts ensue
And we switch roles, each predator, each preyed
Upon by turns, till false and true
Become a whirling pair
Of stars that seem to give the cue
For reason's far and flickering light to fade.

I speak to you as freely as I dare,
Count kindnesses of yours repaid
By thoughts of mine, yet rue
The mask let down, the mind betrayed
When it's our intimacy sets the snare
And your reports of me that they'd
Think no more than what's due
From a crowned head to those arrayed
To strike when new ideas are in the air.

C

I know he fears detection, can't be seen
When foreign dignitaries pay court,
And keeps his counsel lest
Word get around and it be thought
That Monsieur Descartes and the Swedish Queen
Not only see fit to comport
Themselves as they think best
But hold discussions of a sort
That begs some faith-enforcer intervene.

No small thing, entertaining such a guest!
Oh, there were intervals between
Those bad times when we caught
Each other on the wing, broke clean
With old scholastic lore, and made our test
Of truth the will to quarantine
All knowledge that fell short
Of our demand that thought not lean
On props uncertified in reason's quest.

Yet there were forces working to distort
That lucid vigil, that thrice-blest
Companionship, and screen
From reason's gaze the threats that pressed
So urgently on us, that strove to thwart
Whatever insights we might wrest
From that inept machine
The body with its manifest
Shortcomings as our sensory last resort.

RD

Thought shared may stir the passions, and it shows
To intimates or household spies
How frail the solitude
Of intellect, how flesh defies
The rule of reason, and the cogito's
Protective sphere resounds to sighs
Of love and all its brood

Of tricks for turning carnal eyes
From what the eye of reason might disclose.

Alone of all my exegetes she's shrewd
And sensitive enough to nose
It out, the covert guise
Thought takes to hide the debt it owes
To sense, or 'sense' connotes when nicely skewed
To mean the spirit that bestows
On it the gift to rise
Above the thought-disruptive flows
And twists of 'sense', corporeally construed.

Small wonder if I tend to demonise
My sceptic doubts, resort to crude
Stage antics when I pose
Them (always in subjunctive mood)
As dreams or nightmares, scenes we recognise
From lunatic behaviour viewed
Or read about, or those
Soul-torments endlessly renewed
That Dante bids us sinners fantasise.

C

I know, it's Abelard and Eloise
They'll think of, do their best to place
Us in that fabled line
Of lover-savants whose disgrace
In their own time spurred later devotees
To claim for them the sacred space
Of intellect's divine
Vocation, its hard-won embrace
Of truths vouchsafed when love falls to its knees.

I say they're noble passions, his and mine,
Not like that ill-bred congeries
Of body/soul too base,
Too patently devised to please
The earthly powers, that put a mythic shine

Of sorts on their vulgarian wheeze
To build a flimsy case
For sainthood on St. Peter's keys
Conceived as dangling under Cupid's sign.

Much rather think we managed to outface
Those gossips, spooks, and asinine
Court flunkies who'd appease
Their conscience with the chance to dine
Out royally, share false tidings with a brace
Of Lutheran or Palatine
Informers, and reprise
Whatever tales might help refine
Old Europe's plot to sink me without trace.

RD

A Swedish winter, classes on the dot
Of 5 a.m., the daily stress
Of palace intrigue—all
Combined to cause this feebleness
Of mind and body as they jointly plot
That I forswear or reassess
The arguments I'd call
In aid when giving that full-dress
Mind-body dualist thesis my best shot.

Who knows what misadventures may befall
The canniest predictor, what
Disturbances can mess
With the afflicted brain to blot
Those clear ideas that struck the lucent ball
Of mind's-eye intellect, though not—
As these my ills confess—
The unruffled sphere that I'd allot
To pure *res cogitans* before the squall.

And yet: 'Why have this tumult so distress
Your state', she asks, 'or so appal

Your mind that you forgot
How a wise foresight may forestall
Such uninvited passions, count them less
Unruly vagrants sent to gall
The soul in some weak spot
Than guests whose uncouth wherewithal
May give their civil host some cause to bless?'.

C

Your treatise on the passions might have shown
All this to you before you came
To Sweden, singled me
Out, strangely, for your final game
Of wits, this psychomachia where throne
Meets scholar's stool, where your sole aim
Of doubt-proof certainty
Confronts in me the twofold claim
Of thoughts and feelings lived as well as known.

The passions put it in, their plea
For equal treatment, but were thrown
Just what it took to tame
Their rage just long enough—the bone
Of feelings quashed so intellect might free
Itself just far enough to own
The glory and the shame
Of mind by pure abstraction grown
Just deaf enough to passion's shifts of key.

Be clear, my friend: I place no special blame
On you for what I find to be—
As one till now so prone
To count herself your devotee
In reason's cause—unworthy of the name
You crown it with, too *bel esprit*,
Too brainy and high-flown,
If there's more in 'philosophy'
Than fits your mind-and-body wrenching frame.

A Telling

(I wrote this poem to recall and maybe exorcise my four-decade-back encounter with Laura Riding, a poet of great distinction and volatile temperament who took issue with an article I had written about her. The article was a postgrad student essay sent off to a journal, forgotten about and then published—to my amazed embarrassment—four years later. It brought some heavy philosophical guns top-heavily to bear in querying her reasons, in a book called *The Telling*, for very publicly renouncing poetry as a mendacious and self-indulgent practice. That Riding is, sad to say, nowadays perhaps best known as Robert Graves's White Goddess—the muse alternately invoked, worshipped, supplicated, wondered at, and feared in his book of that title—may help to explain the poem's slight edginess.)

No lengthy one, the leap from muse to hex.
What poet knows when wrath may hex his muse?
Her visits may inspire yet put the screws
On all he does, from poetry to sex.

Just think of Laura Riding, Robert Graves,
She his 'White Goddess', he the one whose role
Mixed ardent lover-man with votive soul,
And she the fateful muse whose gift enslaves.

Some things we know: they thrived on conflict, each
A torment to the other, raged no end,
Both switching constantly, attack/defend,
And grabbing every battle-plan in reach.

At length she gave up poetry, decreed
It false, the way of error, language bent
To untruth's purpose; and, lest we dissent,
Composed a book—*The Telling*—guaranteed,

She thought, to settle matters. Several years
Elapsed before a puzzled postgrad took

It on, that strange, self-abnegating book,
And wrote a journal piece, a short 'Two Cheers

For Laura Riding' essay that professed
Great admiration for her poems but
Thought her main thesis didn't really cut
The mustard. Better make your litmus-test

The poems, he said, not principles supplied
By a critique of poetry that takes
Received ideas of it on board, then makes
Their dubious claims a pretext to deride

Such self-inflating stuff. Another five
Years on and, to his shock, the piece came out,
The journal editor (hard-pressed, no doubt,
And short of copy) having risked a dive

Into the reject-pile. Add three years more
And came the furious response: 'I've just,
Belatedly, been shown . . . and really must
Protest . . . ', then sundry reasons to deplore

His briskness, his effrontery, his lack
Of her long service to the poet's craft,
And, she surmised, that donnish ploy to graft
His thoughts on hers, thus managing to stack

The points on his side by a canny piece
Of intellectual gamesmanship. Not so,
He told himself: in truth the thing was no
Such smart-arse put-down or attempt to grease

The academic wheels but more a first,
In some ways raw and sophomoric try
At going ways around to justify
His recent turn to theory. Why'd he nursed,

Of late, no offspring of the wish or will
To write more poems? And—what came to strike
Him later—why his almost Riding-like
Desire to have the giving-up fulfil,

At one remove, the promise poems hold:
That what's renounced, like living-time for time
To read or write, may be the paradigm
Of living-time redeemed. Yet still it told

A darker tale to him, that curious mix
Of unintended outcomes *après-coup*,
Misprisions, and the mischief they could do
When joined, as here, with all the psychic tricks

They play on minds not over-apt to own
Themselves muse-aided, or indeed muse-hexed,
Yet still, like Graves, by turns inspired and vexed
When the White Goddess makes her feelings known.

Verse-Music: ten terzanelles

'The awful daring of a moment's surrender which an age of prudence can never retract.'

        —T. S. Eliot, 'The Waste Land'

Poetry is not a turning loose of emotion, but an escape from emotion; it is not the expression of personality but an escape from personality. But, of course, only those who have personality and emotion know what it means to want to escape from these.

The poet's mind is in fact a receptacle for seizing and storing up numberless feelings, phrases, images, which remain there until all the particles which can unite to form a new compound are present together.

The difference between the present and the past is that the conscious present is an awareness of the past in a way and to an extent which the past's awareness of itself cannot show.

        —T. S. Eliot, 'Tradition and the Individual Talent'

It seems, as one becomes older,

That the past has another pattern, and ceases to be a mere sequence—

Or even development . . .

        T. S. Eliot, 'Four Quartets'

1

Not owning up to much, those words of yours.
Who knows quite what you did, or what the cost?
Not owning up to much, those words of yours.

An idle thought, all remedies long lost.
Your choice reset each consequent life-bearing.
Who knows quite what you did, or what the cost?

Why rue it now, the moment's 'awful daring'?
Rethink things as you will; the price once paid,
Your choice reset each consequent life-bearing.

Vivienne and Emily, two lives betrayed.
You'll live with it, write lines that ease the shame,
Rethink things as you will, the price once paid.

Yours the escape, the poetry, the fame,
Theirs the lost years, lost hopes, lost sanity:
You'll live with it, write lines that ease the shame.

Too late those early cast-offs came to see
What secrets lie in poets' bottom drawers.
Theirs the lost years, lost hopes, lost sanity.
Not owning up too much, those words of yours.

2

The scansion finely judged, the note sincere:
Let that verse-music cast its potent spell.
The scansion finely judged, the note sincere.

It also says you've conscience-calls to quell.
Just use the style you've made so much your own;
Let that verse-music cast its potent spell.

The shifting beat, the low-prophetic tone:
Tact says 'nothing too exigent, too strict;
Just use the style you've made so much your own'.

Let meter and speech-rhythms not conflict,
Have no harsh rhyme betray your *mauvais foi*:
Tact says 'nothing too exigent, too strict,

Else they'll disturb that fine *rapport-à-soi*'.
Stress-shifting keeps those nagging doubts at bay;
Have no harsh rhyme betray your *mauvais foi*.

Meter, like conscience, gets in poets' way,
Throws coping mechanisms out of gear.
Stress-shifting keeps those nagging doubts at bay,
The scansion finely judged, the note sincere.

3

No lack of prudence, that much let us grant,
A lifetime managed like a line of verse,
No lack of prudence, that much let us grant.

Dump rhyme like Milton? Bear the rebel's curse?
Too heretic by half, just not your style:
A lifetime managed like a line of verse.

Much better keep it supple, versatile,
High Anglican, not calling God to book:
Too heretic by half, just not your style.

One thinks: might serve to get you off the hook,
This way of handling things that smooths them out,
High Anglican—some stuff not brought to book.

Back then our forebears suffered faith and doubt;
No style or doctrine offered to provide
This way of handling things that smooths them out.

You'll keep all parties decently onside,
Have verse free up what strictest conscience can't
While churchly tones have backing to provide.
No lack of prudence, that much let us grant.

4

Keep guilt-trips private, feelings safely stowed.
That's how it goes, the Eliotic line:
Keep guilt-trips private, feelings safely stowed.

A weighty, measured style will suit you fine,
Let no unruly sentiments break through:
That's how it goes, the Eliotic line.

Loose rhymes, capacious metric: works for you!
Too plain the feelings with a close-wrought scheme.
Let no unruly sentiments break through.

Else they'd find out, those sleuths of academe;
They'd hear truth's accent in the lyric strain.
Too plain the feelings with a close-wrought scheme.

Ward off those feelings like a shower of rain.
'Style like a rolled umbrella', someone said.
They'd hear truth's accent in the lyric strain.

One hint of that and how the word will spread!
Best play Old Possum, risk no change of mode.
'Style like a rolled umbrella', someone said.
Keep guilt-trips private, feelings safely stowed.

5

Yet if not yours whose words shall meet our need?
They bring us false remission, this we know,
Yet if not yours whose words shall meet our need?

They say: be strong, these words are all you owe,
The daring, the surrender now made good.
They bring us false remission, this we know.

The guilt spoke plainly, told us where we stood;
The age of prudence was a casuist's age,
The daring, the surrender not made good.

'The agenbite of inwit you'd assuage?
Let words redeem the deed you can't retract.'
The age of prudence was a casuist's age.

Why not have solemn speech-act frame the act?
Then feeling good might come of feeling bad.
Let words redeem the deed you can't retract.

Fine words bring self-esteem to swine or cad.
'Keep details vague', the shrewd confessor's creed.
Then feeling good might come of feeling bad.
Yet if not yours whose words shall meet our need?

6

No trick but spotting it lays guilt to rest:
'Ah, good sir poet: there I see your ruse!'.
No trick but spotting it lays guilt to rest.

We (I) go easy on the conscience-screws
When gaps show up in others' truth-accounts:
'Ah, good sir poet: there I see your ruse!'.

Sub-primes balloon as feel-good credit mounts.
How nice to sense our misdeeds part-annulled
When gaps show up in others' truth-accounts.

Insight and blindness: feel the guilt-pricks dulled!
No ducking it, that conscience-boomerang.
How nice to sense our misdeeds part-annulled!

What words can do to quiet the endless pang
May yet rebound as this dark thought recurs:
'No ducking it, that conscience-boomerang'.

You muted the dead voices, hers and hers,
Then penned a line that passed the stow-it test
Yet may rebound as this dark thought recurs:
'No trick but spotting it lays guilt to rest'.

7

'The man may suffer though the mind creates.'
Your take on Wordsworth's passion tranquilised,
The man may suffer though the mind creates.

Don't get the two things mixed up, you advised;
Best fetch a hose to Shelley's fading coal,
Your take on Wordsworth's passion tranquilised.

Romantic heresy, that talk of soul,
As if we cared how poets love-lives went!
Best fetch a hose to Shelley's fading coal.

The mind creates as hybrid brews ferment,
Stray memories, smells, thoughts, images, desires.
As if we cared how poets love-lives went!

Impersonality's what verse requires,
Not self-expression, that Romantic vice.
Stray memories, smells, thoughts, images, desires.

Let feelings not make language imprecise,
You said, like Shelley (one of your pet hates).
Not self-expression, that Romantic vice!
The man may suffer though the mind creates.

8

We see what you'd be at, your coping ploy,
One that could hide a multitude of sins;
We see what you'd be at, your coping ploy.

With those abandoned women it begins,
The style, the doctrine, the entire façade,
One that could hide a multitude of sins.

You spliced it with the latest avant-garde.
Your new poetic fashioned it to suit:
The style, the doctrine, the entire façade.

Who knows what other voices it may mute,
That express veto on expression's needs:
Your new poetic fashioned it to suit.

Long silenced, there's a women's part that pleads
'Don't fall for it, that self-concealer's art,
That express veto on expression's needs.

Too lightly it treats matters of the heart
And casts aside the lives it might destroy.
Don't fall for it, that self-concealer's art;
We see what you'd be at, your coping ploy.'

9

See how you shy from questions more severe.
What if verse-music always pulls that trick?
See how you shy from questions more severe.

The cynic view: 'a verse-finagler's shtick—
Redemption courtesy of sound and sense!
What if verse-music always pulls that trick?'.

The kindlier view: 'why shun such recompense?
Self-punishment: a burden best relieved,
Redemption courtesy of sound and sense'.

Cynic: 'the bliss of being self-deceived!
Pigs, poets, sophists: Plato got it right.
Self-ignorance—a burden best relieved!'.

Too true: verse-music helps us wear it light,
That conscience-call, hold out against the thought
'Pigs, poets, sophists: Plato got it right'.

Yet all too glib your classicist retort,
'No true confessions in the poem's sphere',
Though conscience maybe stirs against the thought
That bids it shy from questions more severe.

10

Plaint, elegy, confession, lyric cry—
Hear how the music soothes the pain or guilt!
Plaint, elegy, confession, lyric cry.

By Eliot's sombre tones or gentler lilt
Poetic speech-acts bring a change of key:
Hear how the music soothes the pain or guilt!

No matter what the mood or melody
We grasp its illocutionary force:
Poetic speech-acts bring a change of key.

Some 'awful daring' drew that late remorse;
An 'age of prudence' went to judge the note:
We grasp its illocutionary force.

Almost the words perform as if by rote,
Retracting nothing but retraction's aim:
An 'age of prudence' went to judge the note.

Two moments, two surrenders: all the same
They show small penitence who show it by
Retracting nothing but retraction's aim:
Plaint, elegy, confession, lyric cry?

Turner: moon and clouds

Somehow I put the clouds behind the moon.
Should plain good sense relinquish metaphor
Or knowledge stifle fantasy too soon?
Take what I need from science, nothing more.
The vision clear, the moment opportune—
Let art not yield to seeing's docile lore!

Make no mistake, they're both out to lampoon
My work: the Country Constables deplore
My raging seas, my 'landscapes' roughly hewn
From warring elements, while those who score
It up to genius always seem to croon
A set-piece from the *echt-Romantik* store.

They hymn the native (read 'naive', jejune
Or simple-minded) gift that has me pour
My soul-storms onto canvas as if strewn
By a crazed epileptic. 'Clouds before
The moon, not mirrored in a sky-lagoon
Behind it'—let them titter or guffaw,

Those critics, still they'd sing a different tune
If they but knew how fierce the endless war
That's waged in me, how what they think the boon
Of my 'sublime simplicity' or 'raw,
Untutored passion'—like some great buffoon
Sloshing it on—requires I show the door

To those (let's face it) sometimes picayune
Effects of mine with all the arts I shore
Against mere chaos—form, technique, the soon
Apparent need that ecstasy not soar
Too high so my sublime takes wooden-spoon
For turning sheer grotesque (my reject-drawer

Will offer proof enough). That cloudless moon
Was like the wild melee of sea and shore
Plus every 'fault' or 'error' they'd impugn,
Those staid academicians who ignore
Whatever truth this gross unlettered loon
May glimpse of man and nature in the raw.

For that's the kind of truth a sheer platoon
Of critics swats away lest what they saw
For just an instant might at length maroon
Them in its swirling depths, reveal each flaw
Of mine a vision-portal, and commune
With all that stirs the soul to love and awe.

Reflection from Larkin

the rooms grow farther, leaving
Incompetent cold, the constant wear and tear
Of taken breath, and them crouching below
Extinction's alp, the old fools, never perceiving
How near it is. This must be what keeps them quiet:
The peak that stays in view wherever we go
For them is rising ground.

   —Philip Larkin, 'The Old Fools'

Look back now and consider how the bygone ages of eternity that
elapsed before our birth were nothing to us. Here, then, is a mirror
in which nature shows us the time to come after our death.

  —Lucretius, *On the Nature of Things*, Bk III, v. 972-75

Otherwise I feel very blank upon this topic,

And think that though important, and proper for anyone to
bring up,

It is one that most people should be prepared to be blank upon.

   —William Empson, 'Ignorance of Death'

Extinction's alp looms large—no smart reply
To Larkin's fearful case, no way
You'll skirt that alp or get
Through to its far side any more
Than get around his set-
Piece, nimbly phrased, yet stark display
Of terror at the thought: I too must die
Like them, reach that base-station, pay
What idiots call their 'debt
To nature', since it helps them shore
False hope against the threat
That creeps up on us every day
And finds some poor crap-babbler's tongue to tie.

The alp's still there in looming silhouette
Despite their efforts to get by
On fake *esprit de corps*
Or tricks to hold the thing at bay,
The thing they can't ignore
Unless it's close-up, eye-to-eye,
And his 'old fools' no longer have to sweat
It out, give Dignitas a try,
Or let soft brains restore
Late calm, now lost to *temps passé*
And too far gone to score,
Like Larkin or Lucretius, high
Point ratings in the mortal-race gazette.

Lucretius, good materialist, said: hey,
Don't brood on deathly themes lest your
Life's finitude deny
That life its joys till you regret
The self-inflicted lie
That had you hold out vainly for
Some far transalpine realm that might defray
Those fears of dissolution, store
Up pie in panic's sky,
And so contrive that you forget
How, though your atoms fly
Apart at death, there's ways to draw
Its sting and find some comfort to convey.

So take a longer view of things, ask why
You fear to think your mortal clay
Returned to source, or fret
That life should bow to nature's law
When death shows up and yet
Have no such *horror vacui* prey,
As rationally you should, when you apply
That thought to aeons past when they,
The particles that met
In you at birth, had yet to claw

134

Together and beget
The chance entanglement of stray
Atomic swerves that bears the pronoun 'I'.

Call those vast aeons from your oubliette
And think, as that last alp looms high,
'Let this reflection thaw
The chill and a good life allay
Those yawning gulfs that awe
Your trembling soul as death draws nigh
And you've not got the gumption to offset
Poor Larkin with Lucretius, vie
For life while Lethe's shore
Still lies a good few years away,
Or count death the encore
To lifetimes lost without a sigh
Since yet unmeshed in living's tangle-net.'

It's Empson maybe had the final say
On death, the sort that shuts the door
On all that with a spry
Riposte that recommends we let
It go, that thing we shy
Away from—sensibly—yet score
Our biggest hits with, poets making hay
Like film-directors. Why implore
The tribute of a sigh
For temple, church, or minaret
When we can quiet the cry
Of thanatropic metaphor
And 'feel blank on this topic', as we may.

Scholar-Dancer

(in memory of Laurence Peddle)

Are we human or are we dancer?

> The Killers, song lyric/title

How can we know the dancer from the dance?

> —W.B. Yeats, 'Among School Children'

Just look at that girl who dances Daphne. Pursued by Apollo, she turns to look at him. At this moment her soul appears to be in the small of her back . . . . Or take that young fellow who dances Paris when he's standing among the three goddesses and offering the apple to Venus. His soul is in fact located (and it's a frightful thing to see) in his elbow.

Grace appears most purely in that human form which either has no consciousness or an infinite consciousness. That is, in the puppet or in the god.

> —Heinrich von Kleist, 'On the Puppet Theatre'

The scholar's gone, the dervish-dancer too;
The curious scholar, Rodin's *Le Penseur*,
And, on the instant, that gyrating blur
Of limbs when tempo-change arrived on cue.
Always they marveled at it, those who knew:
How should twin selves so closely intertwine,
Such rigour with such vigour thus combine?

A false antithesis, so they aver:
Think rather it's the dancer who'd divine,
Absent that tempo, where some latest line
Of thought went wrong, how trip-ups may occur,
Or some missed step admonish him 'you err'.
Think also, as he dances nimbly through
The logic proofs: what did we know of you?

The dance climactic and each thought a sign
Of otherness, of just how far the true,
The valid, and the tenable withdrew
From all that we'd assuredly define,
We 'normal' types, as 'normal'. Why decline
Their promise, those rare moments that confer,
Dance-wise and for the logic connoisseur,

Such attributes on him as left behind
All recourse to the normal, to the test
Of standard scholarship or what goes best
On any dance-floor. Let's say he'd a mind
To think the world afresh, reject the kind
Of sequence, plan, or way of doing things
Where dance and thought are routine happenings.

No cause to think of him as one possessed,
Like saint or prophet, by the zeal that springs
From thwarted genius or vainly clings
To self-belief as if uniquely blest
With such high tidings. Rather hear the zest
That radiates when scholar-dancers find
Steps unprescribed, truth-values unassigned.

His message: there's no stumbling-block but brings
New footwork forth, no error that's so blind
It yields no insight. Let that DJ wind
The tempo up until the woman sings
A proper dervish-stirrer, gives new wings
To body-mind, and drives the single quest
For what thought's body-snatchers long suppressed.

Redeeming the Time: Benjamin *contra* Eliot

A people without history
Is not redeemed from time, for history is a pattern
Of timeless moments. So, while the light fails
On a winter's afternoon, in a secluded chapel
History is now and England.

—T. S. Eliot, 'Little Gidding'

The general point of view may be described as classicist in literature,
royalist in politics, and Anglo-Catholic in religion.

—T. S. Eliot, Preface to *For Lancelot Andrewes*

Tradition is a matter of much wider significance. It cannot be in-
herited, and if you want it you must obtain it by great labour. . . .
This historical sense, which is a sense of the timeless as well as of the
temporal and of the timeless and of the temporal together, is what
makes a writer traditional.

—T. S. Eliot, 'Tradition and the Individual Talent'

There is no document of civilization which is not at the same time
a document of barbarism. History is the subject of a structure whose
site is not empty, homogeneous time, but time filled with the pres-
ence of the now (Jetztzeit). This is how one perceives the angel
of history. His face is turned toward the past. Where we see
a chain of events, he sees one single catastrophe which keeps
piling wreckage upon wreckage and hurls it in front of his
feet. . . . [A] storm is blowing from Paradise; it has got caught
in his wings with such violence that the angel can no longer
close them. . . . This storm is what we call progress.

Whoever has emerged victorious participates to this day in the tri-
umphal procession in which the present rulers step over those who
are prostrate.

—Walter Benjamin, 'Theses on the Philosophy of History'

Almost I might succumb to it, the tone
Of grave, hard come-by wisdom, as of one
'Expert beyond experience', in your own
Much earlier words, or as of young Jack Donne
Already preaching coffin-cased, outrun
By time and late regrets, resolved, like you,
To miss no chance of spoiling any fun
His auditors might think their living due
And have them shuddering in the chilliest pew.

I think of your late summa, 'Four Quartets',
Much cited, much admired, much used to speak,
Vicariously, of those same late regrets
By readers, exegetes, all those who'd seek
Admission through it to a high mystique
Of faith, tradition, Englishness, and all
Such fine accoutrements—the more antique
The better—guaranteed to hold in thrall
Those driven to frequent your well-stocked stall.

Then, trying to dispel the holy mystery
Around those thoughts, it's Walter Benjamin's
'Theses on the Philosophy of History'
That, oddly, come to mind as one begins
To see what's going on, how your verse spins
A mystical conception of time past,
Present, and future on a creed that twins
Deceptively with Benjamin's, though cast
Far back in time to hold time's motion fast.

Not for the hierophant of Christian faith,
Of classicism, monarchy, and such-
Like orthodoxies premised on 'He saith'
As final word, lest tossed into the clutch
Of alien gods—not yours the saving touch
Of Benjamin's *rücksichtlich* angel, wings
Spread wide, storm-driven forward, no crutch
Of faith to lean on, yet in hope that springs,
If not eternal, then from timely things.

For it's the *Jetztpunkt* moments, those that flash
Up suddenly, unlooked-for, in the flow
Of homogeneous time, or cut a dash
Where long defeat and caution said 'Go slow,
Or head straight home'—it's those that may just show
The hearkeners to your faith-centred mode
Of back-fixated vision how things might go
If some new-found old memory tweaks the code
And hope relives a long-past episode.

It's 'homogeneous time' that your stuff wants
To consecrate, a time devoid of just
That brief redemptive interval that haunts
The immemorial sleep of those who must,
At all costs, let themselves not come to trust
Hope's yet-to-time brief visits lest they get,
At length, to kid themselves this mortal dust
Lays claim to a futurity whose debt
To past and present's not redeemed as yet.

That 'Four Quartets' verse-music: what's the tune
If not one pitched precisely to deny
Those Benjaminian thoughts as picayune,
Mere products of his hoping to get by
On earthbound angel-wings, unfit to fly
Because confined by secular decree
To gazing backward at a ravaged sky
While hooded angel-eyes no longer see
Beyond the piled historical debris.

Past, present, future—each, for you, a phase
Or mode of 'empty, homogeneous time',
That sempiternal present that betrays,
For Benjamin, the merely punctual chime
Of history's dull carillon, the rhyme
That comes around routinely, or event
Whose happening lacks the latent power to prime
Remembrance with a charge that maybe went
For nothing once but yet remains unspent.

'Learn to sit still', you say, 'contain your souls
In Christian patience, know that time exceeds
Our mortal grasp while grace alone paroles
This living interval, supplies our needs
For spirit-sustenance, and sternly pleads
We not go whoring "after strange gods" that tempt
The docile soul with God-forsaking creeds,
Or bid us think shrewd counsel might pre-empt
His judgment, leave us sinners guilt-exempt.

For you, the 'still point of the turning world'
Is time suspended, time that's static-still,
Since there's no history but what's unfurled
Past-present-future as might best fulfil
God's purpose, leaving naught for human will
To compass or project beyond the late
Acceptance, on our part, that not until
Our angel lifts its eyes to contemplate
Things timeless can that tumult once abate.

Not so for Benjamin: his angel stares
Back horrified, fixated, as the heap
Of wreckage grows, as every storm-gust bears
Him onward, wings outspread, and as the creep
Of fascism looks certain to hold cheap
All erstwhile gains and thereby to defile
All future hopes—yet he'll be sure to keep
On watch for glimmerings in the wreckage-pile
That flash the signal: go that extra mile!

What's your 'tradition'? Simply one that gains
Canonic power to tell the rest what's what,
The bunch of works that Benjamin arraigns
As barbarism's cultural master-shot,
Its whip-hand that instructs the other lot,
Nay-sayers to that sacrosanct regime,
In ways to voice dissent yet show it's not
So radical or vocal as to seem
Signed up full-time with the opponent's team.

'No document of civilization that's
Not also one of barbarism'—thus
He phrased it, without queasy caveats
Or get-out clauses for good guys like us
Or him, the sort quite willing to discuss
Such awkward topics just so long as they're
In line for culture-kudos or the plus-
Points due to anyone who claims a share
In making culture-clones more self-aware.

Your role? To give thanks as the victor's spoils
Are carried in procession, as they ride
Rejoicing over millions whose toils
Have made that triumph possible, and hide
Its monstrous roots by taking well in stride
The cruelty, pain, and suffering it took
To keep the wealthy philistines onside,
Keep most folk thinking culture's a closed book,
And keep the plebs away by hook or crook.

'This storm's what we call progress', so he said,
That victim of a culture gone as far
As any on the hellish path that led
From Beethoven to Belsen, from all-star
Composers, poets, thinkers to the scar
On its and every conscience left to grieve
At just how deeply intertwined they are,
Those histories, and how far we misconceive
The work of art as fitted to unweave

That fateful pattern. Not for you, his sense
Of the dark signature that underwrote
Each masterpiece, each covert recompense
For brute regimes that had us by the throat,
Or each Arnoldian touchstone one could quote
To pay the needful homage, like those lines
Of yours that so beguilingly promote
A history-lite nostalgia that combines
Verse-music with a tour of scenic shrines

To High Church doctrine, monarchy, good taste,
And—unremarked—all that it took to force
Compliance on the mob. Who better placed
Than you to track that culture back to source
And quit the States for England where divorce
Of one kind or another soon became
Your big theme, from the contumelious course
Of church and state post-Henry to—the same
Thing parsed in lit-crit terms—the split you'd blame

On a deep-laid *dérèglement* between
Thought and emotion such as came about
When schism rose to fracture what had been
Their union up until that tiresome rout,
The English Civil War. And should we doubt
The truth of this, or count it just a flight
Of retro-reverie you're keen to tout,
Then there's your 'Four Quartets' to put us right
By having those rent faculties unite

In a new poet, one who'll up the ante
By picking fresh precursors till the norm
Goes back another age, from Donne to Dante,
And takes the curiously imposing form
Of one whose soul's more troubled by the swarm
Of modern heresies than any blitz
Or thunderclap delivered by the 'storm
From paradise' that Benjamin outfits
With terrors to beware of when it hits.

Your images? A string quartet whose chief
Role here's to match the rapt, slow-moving dance
Of practised partners, weaving each motif
Into that timeless pattern where a glance
Exchanged gives notice players will advance,
Retard, adjust their tempi to maintain
A deep unchanging order, and entrance
The listener lest some sudden key-shift strain
Their nerves or Beethovenian storm disdain

Such playing-styles, such striving to ensure
That history's bland continuum not succumb
To elemental shocks. How then secure
Your line, preserve that sole imperium
From Virgil, Dante, Shakespeare, Donne, and some
Choice candidates thereafter down to your
Discreetly muffled strategy to drum
Them out, those wounded in a bygone war
That fractured sensibilities and tore

A polity apart, then left to you
The task of setting poetry on track
Once more. Yours, too, the critic's slanted view
Of how and why they went off-course way back,
A mythic tale that makes up for its lack
Of documentary substance with a shrewd
Or well-turned catchphrase and a handy knack
For passing off, with po-faced certitude,
Some odd idea that matched your current mood.

'All time is unredeemable', you say,
And make it so by leaving us perplexed
In toils of temporal paradox the way
It left you, reading F. H. Bradley—vexed
Yet fascinated, mental muscles flexed
On puzzles deep enough to tax the mind
Of Harvard graduates—but then, 'what next?',
Except to show how faith alone assigned
An exit-point from logic's double-bind.

'State of emergency': that's how he turns
Your message on its head, requires we junk
That fideist response, switch our concerns
From dead eternity to this, our chunk
Of living-time when only those who funk
The angel's ultimatum need to cower
In the cathedral close of Lowell's skunk-
Hour quarter where the penitential hour
Is that which strikes as gothic demons lour

Or fascists seize their chance to claim a stake
In history. Once dragged to that inert,
Eventless realm no counter-force can make
A lasting mark, no contraflow divert
The storm-tossed flying debris and assert
What you'd much rather have your verse conceal:
The truth that only angels on alert
For fake time-paradoxes can reveal
How they've connived at history's raw deal.

'If all time is eternally present', then
'All time is unredeemable'—they miss
The import there, your readers, though the yen
For thought-subduing cadences makes this
More likely as you turn to reminisce
On past loves, seasons, roses that dehisce
In chapel-gardens, and the sense that you've
Regained, at times, the momentary bliss
That comes of having these high musings prove
The wisdom of your transatlantic move.

Yet ponder them, your lines, and maybe you'll
Just glimpse what Benjamin held out against
In thought's old ruse to sanctify the rule
Of those old powers whose tightening grip he sensed
Behind idealist systems that dispensed
With history, conquest, suffering, and the brute
Or—maybe—the redemptive charge condensed
In Klee's *Angelus Novus*. Battered, mute,
Storm-harried, wind-bewildered, destitute,

And shell-shocked, yet it witnesses how sheer
Endurance through the ages, soul's distress
At body's indigence, and body's fear
Of soul's exactions might one day redress
That worst of wrongs as bodies coalesce
With souls. Then history will give the lie
To those, like you, with voices tuned to bless

The mystic status quo that said: comply,
And you'll have done your bit to satisfy

An order whose transcendent timelessness
Affords an always timely alibi
For celebrants in waiting to profess
The articles of faith, Anglican-High
Or crypto-Catholic (potential fly
In your anointment). You've a wicked ear
For fakery, we know, and a sharp eye
For shoddy spirit-goods, but that austere
Façade lets on what strange gods you revere.

A Rumoured Joy

*If my experience may serve as evidence, a man is more likely to re-
turn a borrowed book upon occasion than to read it. And the non-
reading of books, you will object, should be characteristic of all col-
lectors? This is news to me, you may say. It is not news at all; experts
will bear me out when I say that it is the oldest thing in the world.
Suffice it to quote the answer which Anatole France gave to a phi-
listine who admired his library and then finished with the standard
question, "And you have read all these books, Monsieur France?"
"Not one-tenth of them. I don't suppose you use your Sevres china
every day?"*

    —Walter Benjamin, 'Unpacking My Library'

1

'A rumoured joy, the book that's long supplied
My waking dreams, or solace, or returned
Me to the blissful zone of codes unlearned
As reading lays its protocols aside.

Odd thing, how classics woo me when discerned
Soft-focus, made out dimly, or espied
At thought's horizon just before they slide
From view, those book-encounters long adjourned.

Why think their fabled content can't abide
Our question, got too cheaply, or unearned
Through reading's honest toil by those who spurned
The books for book-chat and an easy ride?

It's all that culture-vultures ever yearned
Most deeply for, what Readers' Digest tried,
Then TV book-shows managed to provide:
A veritable boon for all concerned.'

2

Maybe you'd best look to the books unread,
Tight shut with uncut pages, if you'd seek
The source of all that once conspired to pique
Your curiosity till you were led

Yet further in by every slightest tweak
Of that mind-snagging, quote-entangled thread
Stretched fine through labyrinths where echoes spread
More strongly as the link to source grows weak.

It's on strange waters they must cast their bread,
Those authors, once the classic's high mystique
Allows non-readers every right to speak
Its gist in garbled form, make out 'he said'

Each time some fake quotation lets them sneak
Their own thoughts in, or simply opt to shed
The whole pretence and bid the mighty dead
Just turn the other browser-friendly cheek.

3

Yet might we not, in some small measure, share
The dread that every novelist must feel
As closure throws them back on the appeal
For readerly restraint, for taking care

That author's *vouloir-dire* should place its seal
On how much reader-mangling texts can bear?
Else Barthes and Co. will seize the chance for their
High theory-backed ambitions to reveal

How great are the rewards when once we dare
Assert new rights and junk that crummy deal,
With squabbling readers duly brought to heel
And each book's gist the author's to declare!

An irony: that those with greatest zeal
For textualist theory-talk are those who spare
No pains to mock the scholar-type who'll swear
By textual warrant, scan old texts to steal

A march on fellow-scholars, and prepare
A king-size variorum just to feel
The mastery that comes of knowing s/he'll
Soon shake those rival castles in the air!

4

Truth is, what counts as 'reading' may commence
With some mere bookish tiff but then be cause
Of feuds, resentments, enmities, and wars,
Like differences on how to make best sense

Of scripture, or construe a crucial clause
In legal writ, or hold in wise suspense
The either/or that formed the last defence
Of a state constitution. Then the laws,

Through laxity of phrasing, might condense
Such differences and save us from the claws
Of civil strife, the curse that takes our flaws,
Our want of wit or virtue, to incense

The factions just as *comment lire?* still draws
Much scholar-blood though it's the indolence
Of the non-reader sparks the most intense
Bombardment from their joint-stock weapons store.

5

Still we do those non-readers somewhat less
Than justice if we take this common line,
Make their lax ways the failing we'd assign
To all but our good selves, and so redress

Their fault by having our response combine
Bad faith with self-deceit. Else we'd confess
How often we book-fanciers acquiesce
In second-hand summations, redefine

What counts as 'proper reading', shift the stress
From what-it-says to gist, or opt to mine
The visual memory-banks for any spine
Or jacket that once managed to impress

Our roving glance. Now snippets intertwine
With images and help us second-guess
Which passage of what classic text may bless
The skimmer's quest as need or taste incline.

6

For think how fast, how skimpily we read,
Not least—it seems—when epithets like 'great'
Or 'classic' tell us: here's a book they rate
Sky-high, the best authorities, so we'd

Best pick our option—either allocate
The hefty chunk of time required to heed
Their counsel or allow the call of need,
Work, love, or obligation to dictate

A shorter route-map through the lengthy screed
That now confronts us. After all, why wait
Till Tolstoy lets us in on Anna's fate,
Or the whale's lashings finally succeed

In killing Ahab, or Lord Jim comes late
To face his demons down? 'More haste, less speed',
Close-readers will advise, while skimmers plead
The case for other ways to cultivate

The range of human sympathies, or feed
Not just the stickler's (dare one say?) sedate

And cloistered reading-habits but a state
Of mind that licenses the text to lead

Us adepts from its maze. Then we'll negate
That exegetic bondage since now freed
From any dogma set up to impede
The passage word-to-world, or compensate

For what's gone missing with a textualist creed
Devised to have its priesthood celebrate
A world well lost by striving to create
Some simulacrum of it guaranteed

By terms of art alone. They say we skate
And skip, we non-close-readers, but our speed
May yield rewards denied to those agreed
On having texts offload all worldly freight.

7

Take it on board, we say: books travel, lose
Some valued attributes, but stand to gain
Some others on the way, so don't complain
If skimmers like to play the field or cruise

The intertext, cut corners, entertain
Conjectures on the flimsiest of cues,
Or take whatever liberties they choose
In reading classic works against the grain.

This gets their goat, both parties: that which hews
To 'bourgeois-realist' norms, and then the strain
Of counter-talk that wages its campaign
In terms too cerebral to put the screws

On that old bugaboo. So why complain
If classic texts are those that bring the news
That's always gone before them, or the clues
To issues pre-resolved, like how attain

True wisdom, or which path in life to choose,
Or when to give love's passions a free rein
And when they flag 'beware: oncoming train',
Or any variant on the question 'who's

To praise and who's to blame?'. It's Abel/Cain
The nth time round with updates to infuse
More empathy, less keenness to accuse
(Post-Freud, post-Marx) the faults they'd so disdain,

Those unforgiving readerships whose views
Rose loftily above the creased domain
Of socio-psychic strife or took an Ayn
Rand stance on how to pay your civic dues

As self-made men. Yet, sacred or profane,
It's through myth-tinted lenses we peruse
Those texts as first-time readers, primed for cues
To all the fantasies whose tangled skein

Enfolds the classic.

8

      How not fantasize
About those works unread, those books that lay
No urgent claim on you, that seem to say
'We'll bide our time, we'll wait as your time flies,

Sit here and guard our secrets day-by-day,
While you non-readers, or you time-strapped guys
Who tried skim-reading but soon shut your eyes,
Must henceforth carry on as best you may

With some vague thought of us that quickly shies
From reading's risk'. And so you'll seek delay
Or year-by-year postponement as the way
To head it off and trust to sheer surmise,

To wish-fulfilment, or the passion-play
Of every broken contract to devise
Some ersatz ending or have curtains rise
On other scenes and actions to defray

The cost of self-reproach. They'll maximize
Your chances of a private matinee
With play-text subtly tweaked to hold at bay
Its unknown disappointments and surprise

Yourself, its dreamer, with the whole array
Of tropes and strategies the mind supplies
For having consciousness not recognize
Too clearly what the classics might betray

Too cruelly. So the rapid-reader cries
For untold revelation yet falls prey
To every fantasy that bids them stray
From text-in-hand and lay aside the ties

Of past imagining. What they convey,
Those uncracked spines, is how non-reading buys
Some privacy, some glimpse of open skies
Beyond sky-writer scribble, and how they,

The secret-keepers, scorn to jeopardise
Their world apart by having it obey
School-master lore: let not your set-text stay
Too long unread or yours the booby-prize'.

Talking to Yourself

Is talking to yourself a sign of incipient madness? Consider the dia-
ries of Dr Johnson's biographer, James Boswell, in which he often
slips out of the first person when he's anxious: an effect that's comi-
cal and touching. 'Yesterday you was pretty well', reads his entry for
4 April 1764. 'But confused and changed and desperate. After din-
ner, you said to Rose, "I have passed a very disagreeable winter of
it, with little enjoyment". You was truly splenetic. You said to him
after, "When I recollect, 'twas not so". You are imbecile.' I've always
thought of Boswell as the most deeply human of writers. But now
I shall forever think of him as deeply sane, too: a pioneer of mind
control as well as of biography.

—Rachel Cooke, *The Guardian*, 10th Jan 2021

Truth is I have these moments when the 'I'
Goes slippery, starts to come apart from 'me',
Upbraids me, calls me fool or imbecile,
Has me switch pronouns, think myself insane.

Always that fear: disorders of the brain,
How they can seize the wisest man, reveal
His secret griefs or torments, and decree
His judgments merest folly—what reply?

My master, the great Doctor, source of my
Far smaller claim to wisdom—even he,
As I perceived, was lately prone to feel
The verbal slippages, the psychic strain.

Though dignity required he not complain
I witnessed it, his struggle to conceal
How deep the conflict, how heartfelt the plea
That this dark cloud not spread to fill his sky.

Some vocal perturbation might belie
His lofty tone, some subtle shift of key

Betray the demon following close at heel
To whisper 'wasted wisdom, words in vain'.

Else it's black melancholy, Burton's bane,
That nightly breaks him on the conscience-wheel
Of work undone, all those great projects we
Talked much of as the months and years went by.

They'd say 'The man's a marvel: who'll deny
His scholarship, his scope, his industry,
His peerless prose, and above all his zeal
To judge as truth and charity ordain'.

Yet I, his acolyte, have heard him feign
That magisterial tone, heard his appeal
That Dr Johnson set Sam Johnson free
To track the demons, thwart the evil eye,

But greet the pronoun-shifters, not defy
Those inner voices whose rough harmony
Insists his public self submit to deal
With them, give up its eminent domain.

Myself, I used to worry, think again
Of those bewildering moments, think how real
Those shrewd sub-vocalisers seemed to be
As words slipped loose from that first-person tie.

Yet now at last the answer strikes me: why
Have this thing down as mere anomaly,
Some freak condition they could make a meal
Of in their latest speak-your-mind campaign?

'You was'—so I address myself and rein
The slippage in for form's sake yet, with keel
Thus evened, think 'where any two or three
Are gathered . . . ', till the voices multiply

And I (you) soon join forces to decry
The old concordat that insists 'agree
Amongst yourselves, then all consent to kneel
Before King Self and own his single reign'.

For that requires the myriad-minded train
In single-minded ways, demands they seal
Their thoughts against intruders, aim to see
Nay-sayers off, and seek to overfly

The patch of turbulence that sends awry
Their plan to quell the restless repartee
Of I and me whose banter bids to steal
A frisky march on their august refrain.

Crosswords: Empson to the Reader

> *[The notes to my poems] are meant to be like answers to a crossword puzzle; a sort of puzzle interest is part of the pleasure that you are meant to get from the verse, and that I get myself when I go back to it . . . . And the comparison is not quite a random one; the fashion for obscure poetry, as a recent development, came in at about the same time as the fashion for crossword puzzles; and it seems to me that this revival of puzzle interest in poetry, an old and natural thing, has got a bad name merely by failing to know itself and refusing to publish the answers.*

> —William Empson

The crossword-puzzle interest gives a clue.
I like to do them when I've time to spare.
The best may prompt invention, set in train
A fresh conceit, throw up a fine *trouvaille*.

Only the cryptic sort will really do,
Not quiz-book browser stuff or *faits divers*,
But proper teasers fit to tax the brain
Since standard algorithms don't apply.

It's when you're still on track, still thinking through
Some riddle, that you're suddenly aware
Of words assembling on a tangent plane
With yet more occult clues to know them by.

Thought rhymes with thought, the singing lines accrue,
And then, in answer to the puzzler's prayer
Or poet's need, a glossator's refrain
May strike the listener's ear, the reader's eye.

The Oxford aesthetes take a different view,
Deplore my 'ingenuity', declare
That riddling poetry has naught to gain
Beyond 'the passing tribute of a sigh'.

Granted: their feeling-throes come right on cue,
From love's first ecstasies to flat despair,
And, unlike mine, need no one to explain,
In endnotes, what occasioned them and why.

Yet if the voice of feeling's to ring true,
Not out-of-tune for want of thinking's share,
Then 'Sherlocking' had better take the strain
Of keeping brain engaged and voltage high.

Call me eccentric, but for me the *coup
De foudre*—start of every love-affair—
And sexual consummation both attain
The state coy poets euphemised with 'die',

That sudden lapse of self that can ensue
As much when pheromones pervade the air
As when the puzzler hits on some arcane
Solution with the old 'Eureka' cry.

Solving equations: that's a big help too,
The kind of mental exercise I dare
Say offers thought-procedures more germane
To poetry than much they classify

As its 'perennial themes', the usual crew
Of lovebirds, late romantics, and armchair
Erotophiles who think they'd best abstain
From thinking lest it give their dreams the lie.

The moderns make end-rhyme their big taboo,
Count meter trashed or tarnished past repair,
And take it as their rule: keep language plain
For fear amphibolies should multiply!

I say: take that on board and you'll eschew
Rhyme-led discoveries as rich and rare
As any made by voyagers on the main
Or those with abstract realms to overfly.

It's what those virtuoso puzzlers knew
Whose poems, like their madrigals, took care
To voice no plea direct, the lover's bane,
But use obliquity as alibi.

It's I who set the puzzles but it's you,
The reader, must discern the root mean square
Of all those math-based figures that enchain
Thought's infinite, like non-repeating *pi*.

Once grant us cryptophiles the credit due
And then you'll give the puzzle-poet's flair
For rhyme, conceit and metaphor free rein
For things the lyric warbler might deny,

Like forms that come, as if by *après coup*,
To show what thought-potential rhymes may bear,
Or how clues seem, once solved, to preordain
The guesswork-trail we followed, try by try.

Aerogel: a quintain

Due to their intricate cellular structure, silica aerogels demonstrate great success in impact damping. Dr Peter Tsou of NASA sought to collect a sample of comet dust to understand the origins of our Solar System. Comets eject a plume of particles and dust which give them their characteristic luminescent tail. Tsou headed a project called Stardust designed to collect particles from comet Wild 2. Relative to the probe, the impact velocity of the particles was approximately 13,600 mph. Using blocks of a three-layer gradient density silica aerogel, the probe was able to safely stop the particles, leaving them embedded in the aerogel collector for analysis upon returning to Earth.

—'Innovation in Silica Aerogels', *Innovation News Network*, 21ˢᵗ August 2020

Liquid to gas at temperatures so high
That phase-distinctions blur and leave it there
In place, that fine-wrought micro-scale array
Of lattices the cosmic dust streams through
To layer three, then rests in aerogel.

A sense conundrum: blue as Summer sky
Yet hazy, thin, impalpable, a *clair-
Obscur* of dreamy stuff some latter-day
Tech-savvy alchemist might think to brew
Or strange sea-beast secrete within its shell.

So many wondrous uses they apply
This nearly-nothing to, this light-as-air
Material poised to throw off matter's sway
And do as middle spirits used to do,
From Puck and Ariel to Tinkerbell.

How but by magic get that probe to fly
Close in the comet's wake and track its flare
Of tailback particles, with some that lay
Close-latticed and returned to human view,
Each with its cache of cosmic tales to tell.

The trick's to get the silica to dry,
Shed liquid, yield whatever stuff's to spare
When micro-structure rules, and so display,
In strength and lightness, all that trick can do
To conjure form from chaos cell by cell.

Some hopers think we humans might get by,
In times to come, with new techniques to pair
Carbon with silicon and then convey
From brain to chip all that defines just who
We are beyond the way our gene-codes fell.

Consider aerogel and you'll see why
The plan won't work, how it neglects the share
Of native imperfection we betray
Each time we see in it the shade of blue
That holds us in our sky-fixated spell.

Yet how put straight those vagaries of eye
And brain that science bids we strive to square
With its first rule: on no account give way
To qualities like colour, shade or hue
And grant them space in its high citadel!

Gaze in those lucid depths and then deny,
Should you so wish, that here's the mind-space where
Both realms have standing debts they've yet to pay:
From techne, all that falls to vision's due;
From vision, all that techne's arts compel.

For it's a blue-shift world we occupy,
Dilemma-prone, clear-cut solutions rare,
And clashing viewpoints often held at bay
By hues, just short of violet, that eschew
Sharp contrasts for an azure aquarelle.

Time's Getting On

Time's getting on; the harbour-lights recede;
Each day the profs look younger; journals bring
Reports that some once pillar-shaking creed
Was just a transient rumble, our big fling
At old-guy taunting just the sort of thing
The old guys did; increasingly there's talk
Of publishers and journals vanishing,
While those still hanging on are said to balk
At all that theory stuff. We'd wares to hawk,
You'll say, so why complain?—t'was ever thus
And those with snazzy goods who'd walk the walk
Should view the mark-down without too much fuss.
No avant-garde but soon brings up the rear;
Where now the *dernier cri* of yesteryear?

Silences: Todtnauberg

Although Neumann brings new insights to the infamous meet-
ing between Celan and Heidegger on July 25, 1967, by delivering
an autobiographically coloured interpretation of Celan's poem
'Todtnauberg', he portrays himself as a silent witness, one who
did not just drive his contemporaries, Celan and Heidegger, from
Freiburg to Heidegger's Black Forest hut but who also felt driven to
make an impossible confession of guilt happen.

—Markus Hallensleben, review of
Gerhard Neumann, *Selbstversuch*

Gerhard, they told me: keep tomorrow clear,
Leave off your studies, check your tyres and then
Drive Celan out to Todtnauberg and hear,
If it goes well, how those death-haunted men,
Poet and thinker, find their way to steer
A course uncharted till this moment when
The thinker deems it timely to invite
The poet born to live *in dürftige Zeit*.

I took it on—who wouldn't? that old yen
We scholars have for being first to write
Some charged encounter up—and found his den,
The famed Black Forest 'hut' where they'd unite,
I hoped, to broach the silence that could pen
Them both in its tight grip, the one in flight
From his dark nemesis, the one whose fear
Of a just reckoning dogged him year on year.

I drove them there and listened to their light,
Inconsequential chit-chat—kept an ear
Attuned to things of interest, stuff that might
Make thesis-fodder (I'd my own career
To think of), but the talk was mostly trite,
Botanical or suchlike—just small beer,
So I cut loose, said I'd be back again
To pick him up, and said 'Auf Wiedersehen'.

Two decades on I sort-of keep au fait
With all the scholarship around that trip
Of his, the Jew-survivor bound to pay
His debt so long as guilt retains its grip
And trapped, like some death-captivated prey,
In the spellbinding, monstrous authorship
That seemed to haunt the poet's every word
With thoughts of that encounter long deferred.

One thing the commentators tend to skip
Is silence—silence of the kind I heard
Them both preserve lest either should let slip
Some detail of what passed as I chauffeured
Them back, the poet sworn to bite his lip,
Let drop no harsh word, suffocate what stirred
Within him, while the thinker thought to say
No word beyond what no word could convey.

I harkened to them there, a silent third,
A witness without secrets to betray
Since either nothing notable occurred,
For better or for worse, throughout that day
Of their now fabled meeting, or—absurd
As it may seem—the thinker found some way
For depth of shared thought-venturing to tip
The poet's judgment, have like-thinking zip

The mouth of truth and justice. Often they'll
Ask me, those scholars: what's it meant for you,
That journey back, let's hear the driver's tale
Since you're the one who saw those two guys through
What must have been completely off-the-scale
For silence that spoke volumes. I say: true,
It's left a mark, though nothing to afford
You earnest puzzlers your long-sought reward.

I learned that deep philosophy may do
No moral good; that all the wisdom stored

In those depth-plumbing etymons may screw
A thinker's judgment up; how they accord,
His Rectoral Address, the retinue
Of *echt*-Deutsch poets, and the Nazi horde
Just waiting for the word; in short, how frail
Thought's decencies when savage gods prevail.

And he, the anguished soul I had on board,
The poet, Paul Celan—how words must fail,
My words, his, anyone's, to say what roared
For redress, justice, truth, yet might entail,
If spoken, such a reckoning as implored
That silence end their poet-thinker trail
To that Black-Forest hut. I pay my due
Of silence still, witness each interview.

Femur

I have tried to answer the question which sent me to Samoa: are the disturbances which vex our adolescents due to the nature of adolescence itself or to the civilization? Under different conditions does adolescence present a different picture?

—Margaret Mead, *Coming of Age in Samoa*

A broken femur that has healed is evidence that another person has taken time to stay with the fallen, has bound up the wound, has carried the person to safety and has tended them through recovery.

(attributed to Margaret Mead)

That part-healed femur gave the world a clue:
Behold, our ancestors, a caring breed.
That part-healed femur gave the world a clue.

Cynics and misanthropes said 'pay more heed
To those smashed skulls, piled bones: rough way to care!
Behold, our ancestors: a caring breed?'

Two views of them and us in conflict there:
We nurse and tend, we crush and kill our kind.
See those smashed skulls, piled bones: rough way to care!;

Or else 'the femur, just keep that in mind
And always say they gave it time to heal:
We nurse and tend, not crush and kill our kind'.

'It's your, not their, fine feelings you reveal.
"Let history and science make the case",
You always say: "they gave it time to heal"'.

Why grant those disciplines no human face?
One turned up how the other got her through.
Let history and science make the case;
That part-healed femur gave the world a clue.

Let sanguine types then pay the tribute due:
The femur point we owe to Margaret Mead.
Let hopeful types then pay the tribute due.

It's her Samoan vantage point we need,
Her calm *vue éloignée* that we should share.
The femur point we owe to Margaret Mead.

The insights fugitive, life-changes rare:
Home cultures rule, and so its natives find
Her calm *vue éloignée* so hard to share.

We're all bound up in it, that double-bind.
It tells us: go Samoan, the whole deal!
Home cultures rule, or so its natives find.

But no: she keeps the space-time distance real,
The femur and the shifts from place to place:
No saying 'go Samoan, the whole deal!'.

It's our real-world alternate we embrace,
The culture-differences, the me and you,
The femur and the shifts from place to place,
Us sanguine types who pay the tribute due.

Sonnets for Marsyas

When Marsyas was 'torn from the scabbard of his limbs'... he had
no more song, the Greek said. Apollo had been victor. The lyre had
vanquished the reed. But perhaps the Greeks were mistaken. I hear
in much modern Art the cry of Marsyas. It is bitter in Baudelaire,
sweet and plaintive in Lamartine, mystic in Verlaine. It is in the
deferred resolutions of Chopin's music.

—Oscar Wilde, *De Profundis and Other Writings*

He alone whose lucent lyre
has rung out in the shadows
may, looking ahead, resume
his endless praise.

He alone who has eaten
poppies with the dead
will never again lose
the gentlest chord.

—Rainer Maria Rilke, *Sonnets to Orpheus*

Mixed messages from myth: though music calms
The savage breast it can go badly wrong,
That therapeutic touch, when choice of song,
Or instrument, or auditor brings harms
In place of music's well-known sonic charms
As nymphs declare the prize goes to the strong,
To great Apollo, while the pains belong
To Marsyas, he whose spirit-healing balms
Here met their more-than-match. The tune he played,
The god he challenged, and the flautist's pick
Of reedy nymph-enticer swiftly made
His playing otiose, the judges quick
To have their say: let Marsyas be flayed
And no-one fall for that seducer's trick!

Too easily we think that music shared,
Enjoyed by two, not one alone, must reach
New depths of intimacy, each with each,
And with its joint reward for those prepared
To listen closely, no emotions spared,
Have music mend the fallings-short of speech,
And let its artful melodies beseech
A better outcome than Apollo cared
To grant poor Marsyas. Only think how he,
Like Orpheus, learned too late what perils lay
In music's realm, how fine-tuned minstrelsy
Might jangle ill-tuned nerves till its display
Stirred up such discord as no melody
In his sweet vein could hope to smooth away.

Perhaps a lesson there for those who crave
That Orphean unity of souls, that place
In music's gift alone where time and space
Might be annulled and he return to brave
The underworld once more, deny the grave
His Eurydice, witness in her face
The bloom of youth returning, and embrace
Her living form with strength enough to save
Love's honour in her name. The myth lives on,
But also its reproof to all who'd make
Soul-music of it, liven up her wan
Complexion, lend the Winter's tale a fake
Spring aspect, and ignore its *denouement*
For music's, love's, and simple pity's sake.

Beware those Maenad revels up ahead,
Song-sozzled, note-beguiled, yet set on fire
By lust for his lithe limbs, not lilting lyre,
And glad to see the toy-boy warbler dead,
His body stripped and flayed, his limbs outspread,
Should he once dare to balk their crazed desire,
Stay true to Eurydice and inspire
A hatred fiercer than the passions bred

By pleasure-seeking eros. How ignore
That sanguinary tale, that savage twist
Of destiny where music, love and war
Sink differences and gather to insist:
No melody so sweet it cannot draw
The direst upshot from the dearest tryst.

Absurd comparison, yet comes to mind
Each time we take the risk, when you or I
Put on some favourite piece to satisfy
Ourselves, as soul-companions, that we'll find
That kinship sealed, its contract countersigned,
By music heard beneath the common sky
Of love's attunement where our stars belie
The myths devised to elevate mankind
Above its bestial roots. Time to re-learn
Those truths that Ovid taught: how music brings
Both joy and pain, how shared delight can turn
To shared offence as my soul-music rings
Off-key with you, and how we Marsyans yearn
That some new Orpheus marry reeds and strings!

Postscript: verse-practice, poetics, and 'theory'

Over the past decade-or-so I have largely turned aside from 'normal' academic work and now spend most of my time writing poetry, though often in a form—the philosophical poem or verse-essay—that looks back to my earlier academic interests. Surprisingly (to me) the reception has been stronger among philosophers than literary critics/theorists, no doubt because many of the latter regard it as lamentable backsliding on my part to produce poetry in a range of formalist (rhyming and metrical) modes. I've no right to feel in the least aggrieved about that since, on the face of it, my verse-practice is flatly opposed to positions taken in my early critical writings and represented in the volume of essays *Post-Structuralist Readings of English Poems*, coedited with Richard Machin way back in 1984. Nonetheless I shall put the case, first, that rhyme and meter are resources that poetry cannot neglect without great loss, and second, that they provide the kind of creative-intellectual stimulus that too often counts for nothing in present-day 'advanced' poetics.

I guess one reason for the switch of focus to poetry was a kind of preconscious and pre-emptive strategy for coping with the prospect of retirement. This is not the kind of life-crisis that makes it into bestselling autobiographies or novels—even psychiatric studies—but it does present a fairly daunting prospect to academics like me who have devoted a sizable part of their working lives to the writing of books mainly aimed at fellow-academics. While I didn't want to carry on the same sorts of work—in the genres of scholarly monograph and journal article—I did want (and need) to carry on writing, and preferably writing that stayed in touch with my earlier interests. Hence the poems that touch—sometimes dwell—on a range of themes from subject-areas such as Romanticism, Modernism (literary and musical), philosophy (Descartes, Hobbes, Heidegger, Geach), political theory, literary criticism (including a chatty verse-letter to William Empson), Shakespeare studies, the physical sciences, linguistic philosophy, and the history of ideas. Even the more lyrical and, to most readers, recognisably 'poetic' pieces will often—I hope—ring allusive bells or conjure ancestral voices for those fairly used to such intertextual goings-on. Reading, teaching and theorising about poetry over a long period makes it nearly impossible, and a misdirected effort in any case, to revert to some notional purity of impulse before the cerebral demon struck. The idea of writing a latter-day equivalent of Coleridge's marvellous 'Rime of the Ancient Mariner' is one that has periodically grabbed me but proved highly elusive. Besides, we know from J. Livingston Lowes' remarkable study *The Road to Xanadu* how effectively (if pre-consciously) Coleridge was able to cover his just as remarkable extent of background reading.

My two ballad-like pieces here—'Baffin Bay' and 'Recalibrating'—are very much in the secondary rather than the primary mode, to invoke C.S. Lewis's distinction with respect to genres of epic. Or again, in Schiller's better known but often misconstrued terms, they are instances of 'sentimental' rather than 'naïve' poetry. On the one hand I'm inclined to stick my neck out and say there's a place for 'literary' poems, the kind primarily addressed to readers who'll pick up the allusions, respond to tonal shifts and complexities, register nuances of verse-form, and so forth. In that mood I'd also suggest that stretching the mind around issues of a non-technical but intellectually challenging philosophical or scientific sort is something that poetry is entitled to do and that may help to broaden readers' horizons beyond the lyric, first-person, or confessional modes currently in fashion. All the same I recognise that poetry like mine is likely to conjure resistance not only amongst objectors on familiar grounds of its 'unpoetic' or overly cerebral character but also amongst those—theorists, critics, experimental or avant-garde poets—who subscribe to just the sorts of advanced (e.g., post-structuralist) thinking that I once very firmly espoused. Oddly enough I don't feel that I've abandoned or repudiated such ideas but kept to their spirit while distancing myself from some of their more dogmatic, less creatively liberating aspects. If William Empson, as it seems, left off writing poetry at about the time he started work on his own critical-theoretical masterpiece *The Structure of Complex Words* then my own late-career trajectory has taken just the opposite direction. That is, I have largely given up academic (prose) theorizing for a verse-practice still informed by those interests but now finding them best furthered by a quite different set of priorities.

Structuralism and post-structuralism between them did a lot to put language, especially poetic language, at the centre of critical attention. However, in so doing they excluded some dimensions of language—or discourse—that had long been held in high esteem or simply taken for granted. Structuralism found room enough for formal attributes like rhyme and meter, and indeed produced instances of textual close-reading, like those of Roman Jakobson, that surpassed anything hitherto conceived in sheer wealth of detail and linguistic sophistication. But it also displaced—or sharply devalued—any appeal to subjectivity, whether thought of in traditional humanist-expressivist terms or as the subject-of-enunciation defined by discourse-theorists. Structuralist analyses tended to turn poems into miniature versions of Saussure's *la langue*—language-as-a-whole, structurally conceived—and leave them strangely devoid of animating import or intent. Post-structuralism went even further in its all-out assault on the humanist (or 'bourgeois-liberal') subject as repository of all things shabbily collusive with the reigning ideology of capitalism. What's more, it tended to marginalise any poetry that might contest or offset the lyric-subjectivist emphasis by promoting the values of reason, argument, or open participant debate. The result was a kind of pincer movement that revelled in showing up the linguistically, discursively, or textually constructed character of the first-person singular lyric 'I' while depriving that construct of any valid claim to present a case, discuss an issue, or develop a sequence of connected propositions. In effect this created an odd situation where lyric poems offered ideal cases for post-structuralist treatment since lacking, or routinely taken to lack, the substantive intellectual-thematic content that might otherwise have held out against such purely circular, reductionist approaches.

Moreover, with its literal-minded raising of Saussure's methodological precepts—like the primacy of the signifier and the 'arbitrary' (non-motivated) nature of the sign—into a full-scale creed with sanctions attached post-structuralism tended to cut poetry off from any commerce with issues beyond its own theoretical concerns. This curiously skewed sense of priorities was then carried across into creative endeavours like those of OULIPO in its later stages and the mainly US-based L=A=N=G=U=A=G=E poets. It was evidenced mainly by their fondness for writing pieces made up of little more than thoughts in a vaguely post-structuralist key and identified as poetry only by conventional markers like non-justified right margins. A chief motive here was to get as far as possible from various constraints—of rhyme, meter, form, ideology, the 'transcendental signified', bourgeois subjectivity, etc.—and exploit whatever liberating powers might be found in the 'free-play' of the unbound signifier. This motive went along with a desire to harness whatever elements of randomness might be derived from Saussure's 'arbitrary' signifier/signified dyad and from the semioclastic idea that poetry—or any poetry worth its cultural-political keep—should push that concept to the utmost of its sense-disruptive potential. What went into a scintillating text of speculative criticism like Roland Barthes' *S/Z*, his book-length reading of a Balzac novella, comes across in the L=A=N=G=U=A=G=E poets' take on post-structuralist themes as the belated and somewhat weary rehearsal of a hardened doctrinal creed.

Another factor in my change of mind about poetry was the realisation—however late its dawning—that rhyme is the most effective way to introduce elements of chance that take language beyond the compass of preconceived intent or deliberative prose discourse. I have perhaps written enough about Heidegger for readers to know that I am not here talking about the kind of hermeneutical or depth-ontological brooding on ancient, often highly dubious etymologies held to grant moments of primordial insight unachievable by way of rational thought. Such claims can and do very often go along—as in Heidegger's case—with the appeal to an obscurantist myth of origins and a 'national-aestheticist' mystique of certain languages and cultures as intrinsically superior to others. What I have in mind is the use of rhyme as a creative-exploratory resource which takes the poet into regions strikingly remote from anywhere she might have gone if writing in prose and setting out with a clear sense of topical or thematic bearings. Moreover, it does so while keeping the mind—poet's and reader's—sufficiently in touch with what has gone before to make those departures pointed and meaningful, rather than purely aleatory or (as so often with OULIPO texts) generated by procedures totally disconnected from semantic or thematic content. To that extent rhyme is a portal of discovery, a device that more or less knowingly occupies the zone where creativity in language has its closest bearing on the puzzle of freewill and determinism.

One major source of confusion here is the belief that 'radical', 'experimental', 'avant-garde', or 'advanced' movements in poetry necessarily equate with progressive politics and hence that such 'conservative' or 'traditional' verse-features as rhyme and meter must go along with a retrograde outlook in matters of socio-political allegiance. I was surprised—and a bit miffed—by reviews of my political-verse collections that took this entailment pretty much for granted and advised me to catch up with L=A=N=G=U=A=G=E poetry, OULIPO text-gaming, and kindred means of breaking away from the hegemony of those traditional modes. My response was very much as outlined above: that rhyme and meter are themselves liberating devices and that among the forces they help to liberate are not only those of poetic, intellectual and imaginative creativity but also those of cultural-political resistance and revolt. This they do by setting up patterns, expectations (fulfilled or thwarted), tensions (as between metrical patterns and speech-rhythms), tonal or cadential contours, and the whole set of background norms against which any striking departures stand out. To that extent there is a lesson to be learned from information-theory, namely that the locus of creativity—in poetry as in music and elsewhere—should be sought in precisely such meaningful infractions of a code that nonetheless remains in place as an implicit point of reference. Thinking to do away with the code altogether, or making a fetish of the oxymoron 'free verse', would be like resolving to ignore history on account of its manifold horrors and thereby, as Keynes famously warned, repeating all the manifold errors that led to them. Besides, in the case of political or social-activist verse it is rhyme and meter that best serve to remind us of the link with song—the music of protest—and how effective that can be as compared with the velleities offered by some contemporary avant-garde theorists.

I would thus now want to take issue with Antony Easthope's argument in *Poetry As Discourse*—published in 1983—that meter, and iambic pentameter especially, became a staple of English verse because it did such useful work in covering up the inherent conflicts and contradictions of bourgeois ideology. On this view its fluency and eminently 'civilized', conversational qualities were a means of containing, defusing, accommodating, or placidly smoothing over those otherwise all too evident conflicts. No doubt there is some truth in this claim when applied to certain period-specific examples of the kind. I'm not putting the case, despite all that has happened in poetry from Romanticism to Modernism and beyond, for some unlikely return to an eighteenth-century-type verse-practice where the object is to get ideas and doctrines across with maximum rhetorical force and minimal room for readerly dissent. Rhyme and meter then tend to take a heavily end-stopped and hence dogmatic or smug-sounding form, one with prosodically as well as politically conservative leanings. Bertolt Brecht makes the case with typical brevity and force in his essay 'On Rhymeless Verse with Irregular Rhythms':

> [t]he extremely healthy campaign against formalism has made possible the development of artistic forms by showing that the development of social content is an absolute precondition for it. Unless it adapts itself to this development of content and takes orders from it, any formal innovation will remain wholly unfruitful.

Brecht does some nifty dialectical maneuvering, here and elsewhere, to explain just how his rather clumping version of the form/content dichotomy might yet make room for the kinds of active, interventionist praxis that (presumably) those 'formal innovations' must promote if they are claim social efficacy. He also goes some tortuous ways around to explain how the 'campaign against formalism' can make possible 'the development of artistic forms' through a non-metrical rhymeless verse whose own development requires the suppression of politically as well as poetically salient features of his own earlier writing. Still his basic point may be taken readily enough: no hanging on to outworn verse-forms if their tone, manner, cadence, ethos, or Brechtian *gestus* is such as to block them from addressing current realities or render them complicit with the current social order.

I won't disguise my own partial indebtedness to Pope, Dryden, Swift and other poets in that nowadays highly unfashionable mode of poetry as opinion-shaping or public-argumentative utterance. But there is a change of mode when it is more a matter—in Empson's handy term—of 'argufying' rather than downright assertoric statement or close-linked propositional discourse. To argufy is to make a case and put it across as effectively as one can though in a fairly informal rather than a strictly logical, deductive, or step-by-step form. It implies that there may be other ways of looking at the matter and that a willingness to explore alternatives—as for instance by pursuing a rhyme-scheme into uncharted regions of semantic-conceptual space—is the best since the least dogma-prone course to take. Poets, critics and readers can then get on close, even co-creative terms by exploring the kinds of conceptual-linguistic activity involved when thought achieves some notable high-point of expressiveness, acumen, or self-aware insight. This is utterly remote from Heidegger's notion of authentic poetry, like authentic philosophy, as a thinking that broods on the primordial question of Being as raised by certain ancient Greek words whose original sense has long been concealed by the accretions of Western metaphysics. It may faintly be heard, if anywhere, in present-day German through what Heidegger rather absurdly takes as its uniquely privileged relation to that ultimate source. But the hearing requires a deeply receptive mindset, a passive harkening to that which reveals itself only on condition that the thinker's attention not be distracted by other, less authentic since more busily thoughtful or rationalistic concerns.

I have been putting just the opposite case for poetry in general, and rhyme in particular: that when creatively and intelligently used it sets the mind working in ways inconceivable on Heidegger's account. Empson in *Complex Words* goes further than any critic, theorist, or philosopher of language toward showing just how this can happen, that is, how language can indeed tap into such charged and suggestive etymons while none the less prompting an active mind to register resistances, ambiguities, aporias, or suchlike complicating factors. Along with some brilliantly perceptive chapters of applied criticism the book finds room for a striking rejoinder to Owen Barfield, an Anglo-Welsh delver-back into the early history of words with something of Heidegger's yen for primordial connotations but with a far livelier speculative intelligence and without the block to critical thought put up by Heidegger's oracular tone and wayward etymologising. For Empson, such thinking entails both a drastic under-estimation of human mental capacities and a dangerous proneness to seduction by forms of irrational word-magic.

Clearly not all rhymes are complex words in Empson's sense of the term, just as complex words are not always (or indeed very often) found in rhyming roles or locations. For it is a main premise of his book that the semantic properties involved—the various orders of intra-verbal 'equation' that link the different senses of a word so as to carry an implied statement—are also at work in ordinary language and even in 'flat, everyday' words with nothing in the least 'poetic' about them. What he is keen to show with his examples of the kind, such as 'quite', is that in truth the process of linguistic communication with all its social and contextual nuances is complex enough at every point on the scale to require that we reject any formalist poetics—like that of the 'old' New Criticism—that treats poems as autonomous verbal artefacts cut off from all commerce with prosaic concerns like history, politics, or scientific discovery. Nobody did more to refute all such isolationist creeds, or to put the complexities of literary language back in touch with the complexities of human social existence. However, there is another kind of formalism which sets out to make exactly that point, or to show how poetry handles those complexities by stressing the sheer resourcefulness of its dealings with a language maximally responsive to social needs and opportunities. The concepts of 'form' behind these two usages are as sharply contrasted as the concepts of 'structure' as understood on the one hand by structuralists and post-structuralists and on the other by Empson in his chapters of historico-socio-cultural-semantic analysis. In each case the latter seems a preferable way to go since it closes such a range of otherwise disabling gaps between poetic and 'ordinary' language, poetry and criticism, form and expressive or communicative force, criticism and theory, or theory and whatever it purports to be a theory of.

This is where rhyme makes common semantic and communicative cause with Empsonian complex words: in its power to focus the inherent creativity of language along with the logico-semantic 'grammar' that allows such words to play an active role in shap-

180

ing, expressing, and (sometimes) resisting received or emergent ideas and beliefs. That poetry can, on occasion, do just that—with rhyme serving to intensify the resultant performative effect—is a claim that I would hope to have made good here across a range of politically as well as philosophically oriented pieces. To let rhyme and meter go in keeping with majority practice or for the sake of adherence to some currently prevailing set of doctrinal precepts is to sacrifice a large part of what haunts the sharp-eared reader of poems. A formal scheme with rhyme-patterns sustained over several lengthy stanzas can sometimes, at a certain point, send a poet out beyond the zone of more-or-less obvious word-choices and into a region of new possibilities undreamt of before that point. It is a whole dimension of poetic creativity given up by free-verse practitioners, or those for whom language is conceived primarily in post-structuralist or kindred terms. No doubt this is partly a matter of the differing approaches taken, or experiences undergone, by practising poets as distinct from theorists or commentators. Sound-sense relationships and other features of formal verse are apt to be felt in a far more active, challenging and stimulating way by writers in the process of finding out such creative possibilities than by those engaged in remarking their presence or—as so often nowadays—dismissing them as obsolete. But they are, I think, a vital part of what makes poems work, whether through rhyme or through the range of other rhyme-related or rhyme-compensating verse attributes hit upon by those more sensitive free-verse exponents with an ear for what's gone missing.

Having done my share to propagate post-structuralist ideas that I now find less than congenial I should perhaps say why they once held such strong theoretical appeal. Anyone comparing the state of Anglophone literary theory before and after *circa* 1970—roughly the time that those ideas entered the scene through graduate seminars and a slew of translations from the French—will surely be struck, whatever their opinion of it, by the rapid infusion of intellectual energy and speculative flair that quickly followed. Literary theory, up to then a distinctly marginal or specialist sub-discipline, became not only a significant (albeit fiercely contested) presence in university departments of English or Comparative Literature but a prominent source of controversial new ideas in subject-areas as various as historiography, sociology, philosophy, classics, anthropology, psychoanalysis, and the human sciences at large. However, that ferment went along with a tendency to substitute its own complications and internal debates for anything like the old practices of literary criticism, interpretation, or scholarship. I was as prone to this as anyone, a point noted—often in a tone of gentle but firm reproach—by Frank Kermode in reviews of my books during the late 1980s and early '90s. His lament was that I and other critic-theorists of the younger generation seemed to have lost interest in poetry and headed off for pastures new or disciplinary fields to their minds more invitingly exotic. Empson had a similar though more explosive reaction when I sent him some of Derrida's early texts in translation, hoping for comments I might cite in my Ph.D. thesis. The comments when they came were extremely ill-tempered, magnificently off the point, and certainly not thesis material.

All the same they did suggest that we shall get things askew about Empson's poet-to-theorist trajectory if we take it to show, as commentators often have, that he stopped writing poetry at around the time when his work toward *Complex Words* provided an adequate substitute activity in creative and intellectual terms. That story is probably right so far as it goes but fails to take its own most pertinent point: that this was a switch of focus, not object, or again—more accurately—not so much a switch as a focal adjustment that preserved many continuities with his earlier work, both the poetry and the criticism. What Empson so hated about the Derrida texts—a mistaken impression, based on rapid scanning and my fault for unconscionably asking him to read them—was the detachment of 'theory' from anything like that intensely close-focused and active critical engagement that makes *Complex Words* such a uniquely enthralling book. The continuity I am speaking of also has much to do with the strongly marked 'argufying' element in Empson's poetry, or his flat rejection of the Romantic-Symbolist-Modernist veto on poems that allowed the leopards of discursive intellect into the sacred space of metaphor, symbol, and inwrought structure.

So, whatever the facts about his 'giving up poetry' there is a more basic sense in which—as he once remarked during an interview—Empson 'continued to do the most important work to hand' or, in this context, the kind of work that brought out the fallacy of such ideas. They ignore what he himself didn't have time or patience to appreciate in Derrida: the extent to which critical, theoretical, and creative powers may coexist and interact to produce critical-creative work of the highest order. Though I cannot for a moment claim to have approached their levels of achievement it is largely the example of these two great thinkers/writers—though why entertain that distinction when they have done so much to undermine it?—that I have tried to keep steadily in view from various angles, and across the passage from theory to poetry. The poetry may indeed seem way out of kilter when set against my earlier theoretical allegiances. Yet there is, I am convinced, a real continuity between them, one that can best be approached from both sides and, so far as possible, wearing both items of creative-critical headgear.

(NB: I have not provided the usual academic apparatus of notes and references since this is a fairly informal piece and, besides, the sources referred to can readily be tracked down on Google via author-name, title or topic.)

About the Author

Christopher Norris is Emeritus Professor of Philosophy at the University of Cardiff in Wales, having served there as Distinguished Research Professor in Philosophy and, prior to 1991, taught in the Cardiff English Department. He has also held fellowships and visiting appointments at the University of California, Berkeley, the City University of New York, The School of Criticism and Theory (Dartmouth College, New Hampshire), the University of Santiago de Compostela (Spain), the University of Warwick, and other institutions. He has published over thirty books on various aspects of philosophy, the history of ideas, critical theory, and music, as well as having edited or co-edited volumes on George Orwell, Shostakovich, post-structuralism, Jacques Derrida, and the politics of music. His books have been translated into Arabic, Chinese, German, Hebrew, Japanese, Korean, Polish, Portuguese, Serbo-Croat, and Spanish. During his last decade of full-time university employment he wrote mainly about Derrida, Badiou, and topics at the interface between analytic and continental philosophy. At present his work is focused on poetry, poetics, literary theory, and creative criticism.

Photograph of the author by
Valerie Norris. Used by permission.

CPSIA information can be obtained
at www.ICGtesting.com
Printed in the USA
JSHW080341140223
37667JS00003B/22